CODEPENDENCY

A CHRISTIAN PERSPECTIVE

CODEPENDENCY

Breaking Free from the Hurt and Manipulation of Dysfunctional Relationships

Pat Springle

Second Edition

Edited by
Susan Joiner

Rapha Publishing/Word, Inc.
Houston and Dallas, TX

Fourteenth Printing, Second Edition, 1994
Printed in the United States of America

ISBN: 0-945276-12-5

To my family: Joyce, Catherine, and Taylor.

CONTENTS

Acknowledgments

This book is the result of many people who have contributed to its production and clarity. I want to thank:

- Sandy Ballard, who was somehow able to read my chicken scratch to type the manuscript.
- Dave English, my friend, who encouraged me to write this book.
- Robert McGee, who believes in me.
- Steve Spotts, Ph.D., Melanie Ahlquist, Jim Walter, and my associate, Mark Baker, who gave me insightful and constructive input on the manuscript.
- Jay Hamman, Roger Morrison, and Candy Steinman, who also work with me, and who encouraged me as I wrote the manuscript.
- Susan Joiner, who edited the manuscript and gave it clarity.

Foreword

People are becoming increasingly aware of the tragic effects of dysfunctional families. Alcoholism, drug abuse, divorce, neglect, and condemnation are only a few of the problems that plague families today. Everybody in the family is deeply and profoundly affected by these problems.

Many people are writing, speaking, and counseling about codependency, but very few of them are offering biblical perspectives and processes to deal with the pain, anger, compulsion, and withdrawal of codependency. Without biblical solutions to these problems, people are left with empty promises and broken hopes.

Pat Springle has been a friend of mine for years. *Codependency* contains excellent insights into the causes of codependency, its tragic consequences, and biblical principles for healing and hope. The recovery process isn't quick and simple. It can be very long and painful, but in the end, you will likely discover a positive self-concept, a healthy view of God, and strong and intimate relationships. You will also gain a new identity, new motivations, and a new independence from the bondage of pleasing others. I strongly recommend this book to anyone who is experiencing the pain of feeling neglected, manipulated, used, or condemned by his family. The questions at the end of each chapter are designed to help you reflect on both the pain in your life and the biblical processes for healing. Be sure to take plenty of time to work through these questions. The goal is not "to get through" them, but to understand them profoundly and apply what you are learning to your life. It would be especially beneficial to have a friend or a group of friends help you work through these things. They can provide additional insight and encouragement so that you can keep going even when you are confused or distressed.

Finally, be patient as you work through this process. It probably took many years to establish painful patterns in your life. It will take months to establish new ones. You may even feel more hurt and anger than you ever have before, but remember that for those who have repressed their emotions for many years, these feelings are a part of the healing process. Know that God is for you. It is He who will enable you to experience His love, forgiveness, acceptance, and purpose more fully than ever before.

You'll be glad you went through this process!

Robert S. McGee
President, Rapha

Introduction

Ask a few questions about a person's family, and you'll usually get a relatively bland description; such as, the number of siblings, where people work, and where they live. If you ask a few more questions, and if (and it's a big "if") the person feels that he can trust you, you might find out more than you want to know!

The U. S. divorce rate has soared to about 50 percent,[1] but that figure alone cannot convey the emotional trauma experienced by each family member before, during, and after the divorce. Alcoholism, drug addiction, sexual abuse, physical abuse, and eating disorders are tearing at the fabric of the family. Somewhat more insidious, and equally devastating, is our culture's drive to succeed and to acquire possessions, prestige, and power. We use each other to get what we want, we condemn each other when we don't get it, or we neglect each other in our selfish pursuits. Few families are unscathed. Whether the results are tragic or not, each member is affected to some degree.

In a group discussion about dysfunctional families (families that don't function in healthy ways), a young man was asked to describe his family. "They're pretty normal, I guess," he began. But after he listed the vocation of each person in his family, he realized that those in the group were looking for more than social security numbers. "My father drinks a lot. He's a really kind man when he isn't drinking, but when he is—look out! My mother is really kind, too, except when she's nagging us to stay in line." He laughed at something he thought was humorous.

"How have your brother and sister turned out?" someone asked.

"My brother can't seem to keep a job. Although he's had some really good jobs, he hasn't found one he likes yet. And my sister married and moved to Oregon, so we don't see her too often."

"How have you been affected?"

He didn't know. He was a driven man. He tried desperately to say and do the right things to be accepted by others, but he couldn't see that.

"I'm pretty normal, I guess," he said. Then a strange thought hit him: "Hey, you don't think our family is dysfunctional, do you? We're normal, aren't we?"

Someone replied, "That depends on how you define *normal*."

Many of us from difficult and painful backgrounds think that our families and our lives are normal because we don't have enough objectivity to see our own pain, manipulation, and neglect. This book is designed to help you become more objective about your relationships and yourself so that you can experience growth and health in every aspect of your life.

PART ONE

THE PROBLEM

One

Glimpses

Codependent. It's a strange word. The first several times I heard it, I thought, *That's a very nondescript word. I wonder what it means?* Now, after studying codependency for some time, it still doesn't seem like the most descriptive and lucid word in the dictionary. It is, however, a term that is becoming very familiar to a lot of people.

Most psychologists define *codependency* as an inordinate and unhealthy compulsion to rescue and take care of people. In her insightful book, *Codependent No More*, Melody Beattie defines a codependent person as "one who has let another person's behavior affect him or her, and who is obsessed with controlling that person's behavior."[1] Rescuing, caretaking, and controlling are the central characteristics of the problem, but it usually has other contributing characteristics as well, such as hurt, anger, guilt, and loneliness.

A few years ago, a friend of mine told me, "Pat, you are overly responsible. You try to help everybody and fix everything. Lighten up!" I took his statements as a compliment at the time, but in the past few years, I've begun to see this compulsion as pathological, not complimentary! Many people I meet are similar to me: they feel very responsible for almost everybody and everything, yet they feel guilty much of the time. No matter how much they succeed, they still feel that they can't measure up. Although they try harder and harder, their increased intensity and commitment often result in more introspection,

3

rather than more growth; more compulsion, rather than more joy and peace; and more distance in relationships, rather than more intimacy. It's like the proverbial rat on a treadmill, running as fast as he can, but not getting anywhere.

We need to get off of this treadmill so that we can be more objective and live healthy lives. But growth, health, and wholeness don't occur in an instant. Gaining these qualities of life takes time. It takes a process. And it takes encouragement. Before we examine the causes of codependency and attempt to define it more fully, let's look at some examples of codependent behavior.

Scott is from a small Midwestern town where his father is a prominent lawyer and his mother is a high school chemistry teacher. He has two brothers and two sisters, all four of whom are considerably older than he is.

His father is a highly respected member of the community, but when he comes home, this model citizen becomes a bear. He is often verbally abusive and loud. Scott's brothers and sisters helped each other grow up in that environment, but they didn't help Scott. He was the kid brother; the "odd man out." His mother didn't help either. Even when Scott was taking a terrible tongue-lashing from his father, his mother would look the other way—and get a drink. Her method of coping with the anger in their family was found in pints, fifths, and quarts.

His two brothers took a cue from their father and began to pick on Scott when he was in junior high school. But they went beyond verbal abuse. They beat him and pushed him around. He felt alone—very much alone.

Though he was bright, witty, and a good athlete, Scott could never do enough to please his parents. He looked for ways to help them and make them proud of him, but instead of winning their approval, he was always criticized for not doing better.

As Scott and I talked about his family, I asked him if he had any particularly painful memories. He recalled several specific incidents of his father screaming at him for normal childhood mistakes like spilling milk or not doing so well on a test in school. He also remembered his mother leaving him alone to sort through his father's wrath—no comfort from her! He remembered a particularly bad beating he got from his oldest brother one day after school. And then he remembered the bicycle.

Scott's father always bought each of his children a new bike on their twelfth birthday. By the time the fourth sibling had turned twelve, there were four nice bikes lined up in the garage, and Scott knew his turn was coming. As his twelfth birthday approached, he could hardly wait to get his bike. He had stopped at the bike shop almost every day for weeks, and he had just the right one picked out!

On his birthday, Scott hurried down to breakfast and found a box on the breakfast table. It felt too heavy for just a card that would promise him a new bike that afternoon. He tore open the box and found a football. He looked at his father with an expression of anxiety mixed with fading hope. Was the football in addition to the bike? His father snorted, "I hope you like the ball."

"But...what about my bike, Dad?"

"Is that the thanks I get for giving you a birthday present?" He snarled. "Besides, I couldn't afford to get you a bike. I just bought a new boat yesterday. It'll be here tomorrow."

The boat sat in the garage for years. Scott's father rarely used it. Every time Scott walked into the garage and saw the four bicycles and that boat, he had to look the other way. It hurt too much to think about.

Today, Scott still tries to control his parents' attitudes by doing whatever they ask him to do. He tries to fix, rescue, and help, but he thinks of himself as a failure no matter how well he does. He is plagued by nightmares, and he has difficulty controlling his thoughts. Though he is a tenderhearted and perceptive man, he has very few, if any, deep friendships. He feels very lonely.

When Richard started dating Betty, he could tell that she was a girl who knew how to have a good time! She was the life of the party. Sometimes she drank a little too much, but he'd say, "That's just Betty.

She'll be all right." After they got married, life sailed along for a while, but Betty's drinking began to be a problem. She started drinking martinis at lunch and a couple of margaritas after work. "It helps me relax," she explained.

When she felt bad and didn't get the house cleaned up, Richard did it for her. When she was hung over and couldn't go to work, she asked Richard to call and tell her boss that she was sick. The first few times this happened, Richard did these things with the rationale that it surely wouldn't happen again. But it did.

Betty's drinking got progressively worse, and Richard was giving excuses to friends, neighbors, bosses, and everyone else they knew to cover for her irresponsibility. He not only worked hard at his job, he also worked hard at home. He washed clothes, cleaned, cooked, and he made excuses for Betty.

Richard wanted to have children, and thought, *Maybe a child will help Betty; maybe she will stop drinking and be okay.* Ashley was born after they had been married for five years, but instead of helping Betty to stop drinking and become more responsible, Richard was expected to do more. He had to be both a mother and a father to Ashley. He loved his wife and child, but he became tired and angered by their demands. Then he felt guilty for being angry at his little girl. Richard's life was a wreck!

When they were first married, Richard had rationalized Betty's problem, and had felt compassion for her. But now he was angry. He felt used and lonely, and yet he continued to help Betty and make excuses for her. And he felt sorry for himself; sorry that anyone as kind and thoughtful as he was could be so misunderstood and mistreated. He even thought about taking Ashley and leaving Betty, but he wondered, *Where would she go to find somebody like me to take care of her? What would she do without me? She needs me!* So Richard stayed. He continued to "rescue" Betty, he continued to be angry with her, and he continued to feel sorry for himself. Nothing changed. Ever.

Gwen's father was a successful businessman and a deacon in the church. Everybody in town felt that he was a model citizen and father, but he ran his home like a business, too. He was strict and demanding, rarely showing any affection to Gwen and her brother.

When she was seven years old, Gwen's uncle, Frank, came to stay while her parents were out of town for two weeks. One night, as she was getting ready for bed, Frank walked into Gwen's room and began hugging her. He said, "Gwen, I've always loved you so much. You're so special to me." Then he began touching her in places that just didn't seem right to her. Gwen was startled, surprised, and confused. She was starved for affection, but this kind of affection left her feeling dirty. Frank then told her, "Now, let's keep this a secret between you and me. It would spoil it if your parents knew, and I would be very angry if you told them."

Over the next several years, Frank offered to stay with Gwen and her brother as often as possible. Each time, the same things happened: the fondling, the tenderness, the secrecy, and the threats. Gwen dreaded hearing Frank's voice.

Gwen grew up being condemned by her father and molested by her uncle, and she had no one to talk to. Her initial confusion turned to self-condemnation, and her self-condemnation to self-hatred. She saw herself as dirty, obscene, and revolting.

When she was twenty, Gwen became a Christian. She knew she needed forgiveness, but even after she had trusted Christ, she continued to feel confused and withdrawn. The other Christians she knew seemed to be so happy, and they seemed to be learning so much. In the midst of their enthusiasm, Gwen became all the more withdrawn, despising herself even more.

Sandy's parents had a stormy relationship when she was young. Her father left home several times, trying to find fulfillment in something or someone else, and finally, when she was eleven, he left for good. Her mother found herself with a house payment, credit-card bills, three children to feed, and no marketable skills. A friend of the family gave her a job as a receptionist, and somehow they got by—financially, at least.

Sandy tried to make her mother happy. She learned that saying certain things in certain ways at certain times seemed to help, so she became an acute observer (and a manipulator) of her mother. *If Mother is happy*, she concluded, *then I will be happy.*

But Sandy felt unlovable and afraid. She tried to prove herself by doing well in school and athletics, and with a determination that few others had, she excelled in almost everything she tried. In college, she again received accolades and the respect of her peers as an honor student and star on the basketball team. She had many "friends" because she was clever and witty, but she still seemed to feel lonely no matter how much people respected her or laughed at her stories. The young men who wanted to date her were, sooner or later, intimidated by her quick mind and "know-it-all" attitude.

After graduation, Sandy got a good job in public relations. She quickly received contracts with major businesses, and soon she was promoted. But she was so busy in her successful career that she didn't seem to have time for dating. In fact, men were turned off by her intensity and drive.

A person in her office once asked her, "Sandy, what do you want out of life?"

"I want to be a success, the best in the business," she answered quickly.

"What about a family? Do you want a loving home and children and all that?"

"Oh yeah, sure," Sandy reflected, "but not if it interferes with my career."

Sandy is a lonely, driven woman who is trying to find significance and worth by being successful.

Pamela's father was a salesman for an insurance company and a deacon in their church. He was a workaholic, putting in seventy to eighty hours a week and often on the road. Her mother was a socialite. She was a member (or officer) of three social clubs, and she played tennis several times a week. She seemed to be having a wonderful time, and the couple enjoyed parties with friends whenever he was in town. Pamela was taken to piano lessons, tennis lessons, and every other kind of lesson after she came home from school each day, but somehow she didn't feel as happy as her mother seemed to be.

When she was in high school, Pamela felt sure that a man would fill the gap. Then, she surmised, she would be happy. She had several passionate romances, and soon after she graduated from high school, she became married.

Their passion, however, did not provide a solid foundation for their relationship. Pamela wanted very badly to make her husband happy, but her intensity made the relationship strained and awkward. She became frustrated. She began to nag him, and they grew increasingly distant from each other. Soon, he filed for a divorce.

Because she had received so little love and affirmation as a child, Pamela had never liked herself. Now she hated herself. She became morbid and introspective. Thinking about the wreck she had made of her life, she began to contemplate suicide, but then decided against it. Maybe if she were prettier...maybe that would help. She could start by losing a little weight. Laxatives would help. Maybe a lot of laxatives would help even more....

Allen is a gifted young man who does virtually everything with excellence. He is a good athlete, he plays the piano beautifully though he's never had a lesson, he relates easily to all kinds of people, he hunts and fishes, and he is an honor graduate of chemical engineering from MIT.

He is called on by practically everyone for almost everything. Does your plumbing leak? Call Allen. Does your outboard motor need to be repaired? Find Allen. Do you need someone to teach a Bible study? Allen can do a great job. Do you need someone to play the guitar or tell a story at a party? Call on Allen. Do you want a friend to go camping with you? Call Allen.

He lived a charmed life...until he was promoted to a manager's position in his company. He had always been a diligent worker, but following his promotion, he began working eighty to ninety hours a week to ensure that every task was completed. He seldom delegated any work to the people under him, and they wondered why he did everything himself. They soon began to feel that he didn't trust them to do a good job. It was a strange situation. Allen was overworked, but his coworkers didn't have enough to keep them busy, even though they continually asked him for more work. When they expressed their frustration to him, he withdrew from them–and kept doing his own excellent, tiresome job.

In the midst of Allen's dilemma at work, he married a lovely girl. But like his coworkers, she couldn't understand why he worked all of the time. He tried to make time for her, but his work seemed to always be on his mind. He even cut their personal times short in an effort to do "just one more thing at the office."

During all of this, Allen rarely, if ever, lost his temper with those at work or with his wife. He felt that they just didn't understand the demands being made on his time. But when a new employee became adamant about sharing some of the work load–to the point of nagging about it—Allen blew up!

I asked Allen about the situation and he explained it in detail. (I should have guessed he would!) Then I asked him to describe his family when he was growing up. He told me that he had a great relationship with his father, who was a strong Christian, a Sunday school teacher, and a good example. He and Allen enjoyed working on all kinds of projects together, playing sports together, and talking about a variety of things. "My father was always busy, either with work or with some project around the house. I guess you could've called him a workaholic, but we had a really good time doing many things together."

I asked about his mother, and his expression sagged. "My mother nagged me a lot. She still does. She nags Dad, too. I get really tired of it."

The pattern of his benevolent, hard-working father and nagging mother was being played out in his own life. He lived just like his dad, and he viewed his coworkers (and his wife) in the same way that he viewed his mother: when they nagged—he withdrew.

I asked him, "How do you think your relationship with your parents has affected you?"

He paused for a minute and then said, "I've never thought about it. I don't really know."

Codependency, which frequently occurs as a result of involvement in a dysfunctional relationship, produces a host of painful effects that come in many combinations and take a variety of forms. Many codependents can accurately analyze everyone else's problems, but they can't see their own. Many feel that they are responsible for making other people both happy and successful. They can't say no to any need, or they feel very guilty if they do. They are extremists: everything is either wonderful or awful. Some need to be in complete control of their lives, homes, and their families at all times; others have given up on life, and are irresponsible and out of control.

All codependents, when they are honest with themselves, feel that they are unworthy of love and acceptance. For many, however, gaining objectivity is a long, slow process. At first, they may not even feel this kind of hurt at all because their defense mechanism of denial is so strong.

Of the myriad characteristics that many codependents seem to share, six prevail as a basis for all the others. The first three are the *primary* characteristics of codependency:

1. A lack of objectivity
2. A warped sense of responsibility
3. Being easily controlled and controlling others

The next three are common *corollary* characteristics, or side effects, of codependency:

4. Hurt and anger
5. Guilt
6. Loneliness

(Of course, this does not mean that every person who feels angry or guilty is necessarily codependent. This list of characteristics signifies that a person who experiences the first three—the primary characteristics of codependency—may well experience hurt and anger, guilt, and loneliness as well.)

Are you codependent? Do you have a family member or a friend who is codependent? How do codependents get help?

This book is designed to help "turn the lights on" in your life so that you will *understand* yourself and say, "*That's* why I feel this way! *That's* why I act this way!" The first section of this book gives much attention to the problems and pain of codependency, but its purpose is not to promote self-pity. Its purpose is to promote objectivity, reality, and godly independence. The analysis of the problem is only the first part of the process toward healing.

With understanding comes *hope for change.* You don't have to stay in the grip of codependency for the rest of your life!

With understanding and hope, you can begin (or continue) a *process* toward spiritual, emotional, and relational health. These changes aren't instantaneous, but they are possible.

For many of us, the light, the sense of hope, and the stability, intimacy, and vitality in our lives has been blocked out by codependency like the light of the sun blocked by an eclipse. But just as the light of the sun slowly begins to emerge after its darkest moment, the light of Christ can begin to emerge in our lives, too. We can have a sense of hope, a sense of stability, a sense of worth, and a sense of intimacy in our relationships with others—and in our relationship with God.

Two

The Cause of Codependency

Codependency is not just a set of isolated feelings or behaviors. It is not a surface problem. Consequently, superficial solutions don't help. A deep hurt—an unmet need for love and acceptance—either numbs the codependent or drives him to accomplish goals so he can please people and win their approval. Codependent emotions and actions are designed to blunt pain and gain a desperately needed sense of worth. The problem with codependent behavior is that it yields only short-term solutions which ultimately cause more pain.

God has a different plan; a plan for stability and security; a plan for love, protection, and provision. Dysfunctional families, however, wreck this plan and produce the pain, numbness, drive, and defense mechanisms characterized by codependency.

God's Design for the Family

The Lord created and designed the family as the primary environment for our experience of His love and strength. The husband-wife relationship and the parent-child relationship are intended to be reflections and models of our relationship with God. The function (or dysfunction) of these relationships shapes each family member's view of God and his self-concept.

The husband is instructed to cherish his wife, to take time to understand her, provide for her, enjoy her, and love her in the same way that Christ does for His people (Eph. 5:25-33; 1 Pet. 3:7; Col. 3:19; Prov. 5:15-19). In response to this strong and tender love, the wife is to respect her husband, enjoy her relationship with him, and develop her own identity and skills as she helps to provide for the family's needs (Eph. 5:22-33; 1 Pet. 3:1-6; Col. 3:18; Prov. 31:10-31). The husband and wife are to be an intimate unit with a common purpose, but with distinct identities and roles.

Most children flourish in this kind of loving and strong environment (though in the complex world of relationships, some children fail to flourish in very positive environments, while some become stable and healthy even if their families haven't been). In the family that follows God's design, children are highly valued (Ps. 127:3; Mark 9:36; 10:15). They receive compassion for their hurts and disappointments (Ps. 103:13), loving correction and discipline (Prov. 13:24), forgiveness and acceptance (Luke 15:11-24), patient and persistent instruction (Deut. 6:6-9), and understanding in the context of love and direction (Eph. 6:4; Prov. 22:6).

Consistent, loving discipline is tremendously important to the development of children. Without it, they have no boundaries, no clean sense of right and wrong, and they are forced either to discipline themselves or suffer the discipline of an authority who primarily wants to restrict their destructive behavior. Receiving loving discipline as a child prevents many interpersonal and intrapersonal difficulties throughout life.

So then, children need a balance of both love and limits. They need affirmation, warmth, comfort, attention, and time so they will believe that they are valuable, special people. They also need a clear understanding of what is right and wrong. They need loving discipline. They need to understand the consequences of their behavior, and as they grow up, they need for their parents to impart convictions and values so that they can be weaned from external discipline. Then, appropriate limits will be internalized in their lives.

Both parents have a role in providing this environment. Some people, however, think that the mother is supposed to be tender and the father is supposed to be tough, but this is an incorrect view of the separate parental roles under God's design. *Both* are to be tender and compassionate (Luke 15:4-24; Ps. 103:13; Gen. 25:28; Exodus 2; 1 Thess. 2:7, 11) and *both* are to be strong (Prov. 13:24; 31:10-31; Eph. 6:4).

Harvard professor, Nicholi Armand, explained the importance of both parents in a child's development:

> *If one factor influences the character development and emotional stability of a person, it is the quality of the relationship he experiences as a child with both of his parents. Conversely, if people suffering from severe non-organic emotional illness have one experience in common, it is the absence of a parent through death, divorce, a time-demanding job, or absence for other reasons.*[1]

Dysfunctional Families

Selfishness has been a deterrent to stable, loving families since the beginning of man's history. Strong and loving families are becoming rare in our culture. The insatiable thirst for personal success and self-indulgent pleasures distorts God's design for the family. Selfishness replaces unconditional love in both husband-wife and parent-child relationships. We value positions, possessions, and pleasure. Spouses and children who interfere with our pursuits are considered nuisances; so much so that divorce has grown to epidemic proportions. Between 1960 and 1980, the divorce rate jumped from nine to twenty-three for every 1,000 women, a 255 percent increase in only twenty years. As a result, families are dysfunctional; that is, they do not function in the way that God intended. They do not provide the security, love, and acceptance that all people so desperately need.

Some studies attempt to demonstrate the positive effects of divorce on children, stating that they become more independent, learn how to interact with extended step-families, and are thus less selfish.[2] Other researchers point to the ability of children to bounce back from the stress of divorce.[3] But most people (85 percent) are convinced that divorce is hard on children. Even divorcees say so, by more than a seven out of ten margin.[4]

This suspicion is evidenced by other studies which show strong, negative effects upon children of divorce. For example, children of divorce show signs of stress: they are more emotionally troubled; the fear of divorce affects their love lives; they are forced to act as adults while still in their pre-teens (e.g., assuming adult responsibilities, comforting and caring for their divorced parents, caring for younger children without adult supervision). When parents remarry, this stress is compounded (due to the death of the dream that mom and dad will get back together).[5,6]

Divorce is only one type of family dysfunction that has devastating effects on spouses and children. The stability and affection that all of them need are battered and eroded by the stress, anger, and hurt that lead to separation. These are usually replaced by some relief, but also by guilt, bitterness, and loneliness after the divorce. It's not a very beneficial swap.

In every dysfunctional family, there is both the presence of some painful characteristics and the corresponding absence of some needed characteristics. Attributes found in dysfunctional families may include:

alcoholism
drug addiction
workaholism
divorce
eating disorders
sexual disorders
absent father
absent mother

neglect

verbal abuse

emotional abuse

physical abuse

sexual abuse

domineering father/passive mother

domineering mother/passive father

After studying alcoholism and drug addiction, Dr. Joseph A. Pursch, of the Family Care Clinic in Santa Ana Heights, California, observed, "We know that the average affected family consists of 1.8 alcoholics/addicts and four codependents."

In dysfunctional families, there is an absence of (or, at least, too little of) the qualities that people need to become healthy and secure:

unconditional love

unconditional acceptance

forgiveness

laughter

fun

a sense of worth

time to work and play together

attention

compassion

comfort

honesty

objectivity

freedom to express emotions appropriately

friendship

freedom to have your own opinion, your own identity

appropriate responsibility

loving correction

affirmation

To the degree that the development of these characteristics is hindered, the members of the family are hindered in their spiritual, emotional, and relational well-being. Among the many maladies in dysfunctional families is the compulsion to rescue, fix, and control people and situations, i.e., codependency.

Obviously, no family is perfect, but perfection is not the goal of family relationships. Relationships that are real, genuine, and honest—and that offer the freedom to express true feelings—are far better than perfectionism. We all suffer from the devastating effects of sin, but families can at least provide some of the love, protection, and provision each of its family members so desperately needs.

The painful consequences of dysfunctional behavior in families are many and varied. A young girl from an alcoholic home seeks the love and affection she never got from her parents by going from one lover to another. But her empty feeling inside remains. The wife of a drug addict tries desperately to help him by making excuses for him and getting a job because he wastes so much money on pills. She is furious, but she just smiles and says, "That's all right, honey. I don't mind." An executive pours his life into his job and gets promotion after promotion just to prove to his parents that he is worthy of their respect. An elderly widow, whose husband was addicted to prescription drugs and committed suicide, expects her children to provide for her every need. They do, but she still nags them constantly, and none of them are happy. A college student is called "spacey" because she never seems able to pay attention. No one realizes that she was sexually abused as a child. Her drive to fix her parents' shaken marriage has been coupled with an abject fear of her father. She continues to feel that she is repulsive and dirty, and has withdrawn from everyone around her in a defensive attempt to block the pain. A youth pastor is very disciplined in his personal life and expects (demands) the high school students involved in his program to be just as committed and disciplined as he is. He is often disappointed at their "immaturity and rebellion" for not doing all that he has asked them to do. He appears to be the epitome of confidence and security, but secretly he wonders if his mother was right. She told him a hundred times, "You won't amount to anything!"

Tragically, the painful consequences of dysfunctional families do not end with the children. The law of sowing and reaping indicates that these consequences will be duplicated in generation after generation (Ex. 20:5) until either the original offense is diluted, or until someone has the insight and the courage necessary to change the course of his family's history.

The Need to Be Loved/The Need to Feel Valued

All people are created with a God-given need to be loved and to have a sense of worth. It is God's intent that these needs be met by two primary sources: the grace of God through Christ and the reflection of His grace and strength in the family. These two sources are not meant to function separately, but are intended to form a cohesive environment. The content of the Gospel will have fertile soil when the character of God is modeled by the parents.

It is difficult to overestimate the influence of the family in a person's development. A child can grow up in a home where the parents are Christians, but are too strict, critical, or neglectful (all types of dysfunctional attributes can exist in Christian families). The result will be a hurting, guilt-ridden, driven, overly responsible, or completely passive person; that is, a codependent. On the other hand, a child can be nurtured and protected in a home where the parents aren't believers. The warmth, affection, attention, and strength in this family will be much more likely to produce a stable and secure child than in a codependent, Christian household. This may sound like heresy to some people, but children don't care a lot about theology. They care about being loved—*really* loved, not just in words but in deeds—with time, attention, and affection. They need time to relax, study, and play together; to be listened to and comforted when they hurt, and praised when they do well. Parents can do that. Empty theology can't.

When a person lives in an environment of love and acceptance, he tends to blossom. In dysfunctional families, where these basic needs aren't met, people are left to find other avenues to meet those pressing needs. The compelling goal of their lives becomes having those needs met. Everything they say or do is consciously or unconsciously designed to numb their pain and gain a sense of intimacy with others and a sense of worth in their own eyes. Some escape to passivity. Some are driven to succeed to prove their worth. Most of us do both in varying combinations. Some aspects of codependency are pitiful. Codependency crushes a person. It crushes his stability and his identity. It keeps him from enjoying all that God has for him. According to some psychiatrists and psychologists, the crushing nature of codependency does its awful work in the majority of people when they are most vulnerable: while they are young children. The eminent Harvard physician and child psychiatrist, Dr. Burton White, has found that in the first three years of a child's life, the home environment is critical. If those years are full of warmth, love, and protection, the child will probably develop a very healthy self-concept and a healthy view of life. If, however, a child grows up in a dysfunctional family, he will be deprived of these necessities to some degree, and his emotional and relational health will be adversely affected for the rest of his life. Dr. White does not take into account the power of God's Spirit to change lives, but his point is well taken: it is extremely difficult for a child to change his self-concept after the age of three! [7]

Codependents long to be loved. They desperately want to have a sense of worth and specialness. Those needs are God-given, but in a codependent family, the resources to meet those needs have often been withheld.

The Cause of Codependency

Perhaps a chart will help explain both the cause and the effects of codependency. In the following, the God-given needs for love, security, worth, protection, and provision are presented first. Then, two possible environments are listed: one for a functional family and one for a dysfunctional family, with corresponding effects or consequences of each. The chart concludes with the motivational patterns that healthy and codependent people develop.

Needs	Environment	Results	Motivation
Love Security Worth	**Functional Family:** love, acceptance, forgiveness, protection, provision, honesty, freedom to feel, loving discipline	**Spiritual, emotional, relational health:** love, anger, fear, laughter, intimacy, willingness to take risks	**Healthy Motives:** love, thankfulness, obedience out of gratitude
Protection Provision	**Dysfunctional Family:** (alcoholism, drug abuse, eating disorders, etc.): condemnation, rejection, destructive criticism, manipulation, neglect, abuse, unreality, denial	**Codependency:** lack of objectivity, warped sense of responsibility, controlled/controlling, guilt, hurt and anger, loneliness	**Compulsive Motives:** avoid pain, fear of rejection, fear of failure, gain a sense of worth, accomplish goals to win approval

Too often, we look at the behavior and emotions of codependency—either in ourselves or other people—and try to "fix" them without examining their cause. Hopefully, this chart will help you see that there is a very clear cause.

A Definition

Codependency was coined in the 1970s in the context of treating alcoholism. Alcoholics were observed to share a somewhat consistent set of behaviors. As therapists treated families of these alcoholics, they observed that the family members also exhibited a fairly consistent pattern of behavior. The alcoholic was *dependent* on alcohol. The family was affected, too, so they were called *codependent*.

Originally, *codependent* was applied to the families of alcoholics. Later, the term was given to families of those who were dependent on any kind of drug, including alcohol. Today the word is used to describe anyone in a significant relationship with a person who exhibits any kind of dependency. Some of these dependencies are more subtle than others, and may include alcohol, drugs, sex, food, work, gambling, perfectionism, success, etc. Those who are adversely affected by the dependent person's behavior; who have an imbalanced sense of responsibility to rescue, fix, and/or help the dependent person are codependent. The dependent person either consciously or unconsciously deprives the codependent of needed love and attention. This provokes *rescuing* as a means of obtaining that affirmation.

One young man I know has parents who, by all appearances, seem to be stable though his mother is demanding and his father is passive. This young man doesn't think of his family as being dysfunctional, yet in response to their behavior, he is driven to "fix" their problems and those of everyone around him. A woman from a divorced home feels that it is her responsibility to "rescue" her mother and make her mother happy. But in response to her mother's behavior, she feels like a failure.

Neither of these families is characterized by alcoholism or drug abuse, but both the young man and the woman are compulsive fixers and helpers. To some degree, they both are codependent because of their drive to rescue.

Everybody, it seems, has his own definition of codependency. Here are some examples:

- Codependency is bondage to pleasing somebody.
- It is being controlled by someone and trying to control him or her.
- It is being dependent on making someone else happy.
- Codependency is the responsibility to make others happy, successful, and good.
- It is a hurting child in an adult's body.

- It is feeling guilty when you don't do everything just right—and that's all the time!
- Codependency is trying to make a sick person well, but ending up sick yourself!

As we have seen, at the root of codependency is a relationship with a dysfunctional person which results in an unmet need for love and security. A person may be born into a dysfunctional family where one of the parents is an alcoholic, a workaholic, is abusive, or suffers from some other form of abnormal and/or destructive behavior. Or a person may be relatively healthy, but marry someone who is dysfunctional. That type of relationship can sap a normally secure person of his sense of stability and self-confidence, resulting in codependent behavior. This can happen through many types of relationships. A college freshman can move into a dorm room with a dysfunctional person. A troubled family may move next door to a compassionate housewife and take advantage of their well-meaning neighbor. She, too, may become codependent through this new relationship.

Whatever the source and whatever the cause, codependency involves a relationship with a dysfunctional, addicted, or troubled person. The closer the relationship, the younger the age, and the more time that is spent together, the greater the degree of codependency. Too often, the victim of an alcoholic becomes an alcoholic himself. The codependent victim of a dysfunctional agent becomes an agent, too, and the cycle continues.

We will define codependency this way: *Codependency is a compulsion to control and rescue others by fixing their problems.* It occurs when a person's God-given needs for love and security have been blocked in a relationship with a dysfunctional person, resulting in a lack of objectivity, a warped sense of responsibility, being controlled and controlling others (the three primary characteristics named in chapter 1); and in hurt and anger, guilt, and loneliness (the three corollary characteristics). This affects the codependent's every relationship and desire. His goal in life is to avoid the pain of being unloved and to find ways to prove that he is lovable. It is a desperate quest.

Some have asked, "Aren't *all* people codependent?" No, they aren't. All people have experienced the effects of sin and, to a degree, share the misery of these six characteristics, but codependents experience these difficulties at a much greater level.

How do you know if you're codependent? First, look at your relationships, then at your symptoms. The rule of thumb is this: If you are in a relationship with someone who is addicted, abusive, neglectful, or condemning, and if you feel that you are responsible for making him happy, then you are most probably codependent. Examine your symptoms. As you look at the six characteristics in the next several chapters, and if you feel that these (or at least the first three) describe you to a significant degree, then you are probably codependent. Even if your parents, your spouse, or your children do not have abusive or addictive disorders, it may be that you are a second- or third-generation codependent. Perhaps your grandparents or great-grandparents had these kinds of disorders, and the effects are still being felt in the family.

Are we saying that codependents are terrible people? Certainly not! Codependents are some of the most generous, sensitive, bright, articulate, efficient, effective, and wonderful people on earth. But they are hurting, lonely people who desperately want to be loved. Consequently, they try to fix people and things. They try to make others happy without thinking of their own happiness, allowing themselves to be controlled by the praise and condemnation of others, while also trying to control their own lives. Codependents give up their own identity, their own ideas, and their own emotions and force themselves instead to feel and act in a way that pleases other people. Why? Because they so desperately want to be loved. Ultimately, these coping behaviors don't work. No matter how hard they try (and some try so hard that they have emotional and/or physical breakdowns, while others give up and escape into their own world of self-indulgence), their needs for love, worth, and significance go unmet.

Superficial solutions to codependency don't work either. As we grow up, our family relationships provide each of us with perceptions comparable to a pair of glasses through which we see ourselves and the world. Some of us have a clear pair of glasses that allows us to see reality, both its good and bad, because we are secure enough to handle that reality. But a codependent person has a pair of glasses that distort reality, so that even the good things in life often seem bad. These glasses need to be modified, but to alter them, we must take the time to understand what has happened to us and begin the *process* of change, no matter how long it takes. We will take a long, hard look at the six painful characteristics of codependency, but first, take a few moments to answer the following questions. They will help you gain a better picture of your tendencies toward codependency.

Questions

The following questions are taken from a helpful analysis of adult children of alcoholics, but they are applicable for all codependents. Answer the following:

1. Do I often feel isolated and afraid of people, especially authority figures?

2. Have I observed myself to be an approval-seeker, losing my own identity in the process?

3. Do I feel overly frightened of angry people and personal criticism?

4. Do I often feel I'm a victim in personal and career relationships?

5. Do I sometimes feel I have an overdeveloped sense of responsibility, which makes it easier to be more concerned with others than with myself?

6. Is it hard for me to look at my own faults and my own responsibility to myself?

7. Do I feel guilty when I stand up for myself instead of giving in to others?

8. Do I feel addicted to excitement?

9. Do I confuse love with pity, and tend to love people I can pity and rescue?

10. Is it hard for me to feel or express feelings, including feelings such as joy or happiness?

11. Do I judge myself harshly?

12. Do I have a low sense of self-esteem?

13. Do I often feel abandoned in the course of my relationships?

14. Do I tend to be a reactor instead of an initiator?

• Write a paragraph to describe what your responses to these questions tell you about yourself:

15. How has your family influenced your self-concept, your perception of others, and your perception of God? (See the exercises in Appendixes A–F on pages 263 to 285 for answers to this question.)

Three

Lack of Objectivity

Ken asked me to visit with him and his wife, Helen, over lunch. As we talked, Ken said that Helen had been feeling guilty and depressed since their previous visit with her parents. She explained, "Our last time with my parents was hard. My mother was very critical of me, and even of our children. I've felt really guilty since we left there."

"Tell me about your parents," I probed.

"My father is a wonderful man. He's loving and very supportive of me. My mother does a lot for me; she's very protective, but sometimes, she can be kind of critical."

"Sometimes?" Ken looked at Helen.

"Okay, more than sometimes."

I asked, "What has your mother been critical of?"

Helen thought, and looked away as she answered, "When I was growing up, she criticized how I looked, the clothes I wore, my friends, my grades. Now she's critical of my husband, my children...just about everything."

"How does your father respond when your mother criticizes you?"

"Oh, he goes into the living room and reads the paper. That's the way he copes when she nags him—which is just about all the time." She smiled weakly. "Daddy spends a *lot* of time in the living room reading the paper."

"How do you respond to your mother, Helen?"

"Well, I've always tried to make her happy. I've always tried to please her, but I guess I just haven't been the daughter she wants me to be. "I've really tried, though." Her voice trailed off.

"Helen, how did you, or how do you feel when your mother criticizes you?"

"Well, guilty, I guess...guilty that I can't make her happy, that I've failed as her child."

"How does she treat your children?"

"Just like she treats me. Her criticism has never bothered me, but I don't want her to treat my children that way! I just don't know how to get her to treat us well." Her voice was trailing off again as she looked down. I asked, "Do you think your mother has been loving toward you in all of this?"

Helen looked stunned. "Of course!"

"Do you show love that way, Helen?"

"No, (pause) but I know my mother loves me no matter what I do."

"How?"

"Well...I guess I...I've just assumed that she loves me."

I could tell that Helen was offended by my questions about her mother's love for her. We finished lunch with some small talk and then graciously parted.

A few days later, Helen phoned me. She wanted to talk again, so I met her and Ken for coffee.

Helen began, "Maybe you're right. Maybe...but I hurt so bad, I feel so guilty all the time...but I just *know* she loves me." Helen began to cry. Ken put his arm around her.

I asked her, "Have you ever felt angry with your mother when she is being critical of you?"

"No...no, I haven't."

"Why not?" I asked, "Wouldn't anger be a normal response to someone who has condemned you, to someone who has hurt you?"

"Well...I guess so."

"Helen, how would you want your mother to treat you?"

Her eyes brightened. (She had obviously dreamed of this many times.) "She would affirm me, love me even if I'm overweight, talk to me (not *at* me), listen to me. We'd be friends. We'd do fun things together." A pause, then, "She wouldn't slam the door of my room and leave me crying all alone."

Helen raised her voice, "But she never did those kind and thoughtful things! Never! She always made me wear the clothes *she* picked out for me. Even in high school."

Then Helen broke into uncontrollable weeping. Ken asked her gently, "What is it, honey?"

Helen looked up through her tears and sobbed, "She even made me take back a gown I'd bought for a big party. She made me wear one that *she* picked out. It was horrible! Everybody laughed at me!" Her voice calmed. "I haven't thought of that in years."

Through several more conversations, Helen started getting in touch with her deep hurt and repressed anger. It was the beginning of objectivity. It was the beginning of healing.

Helen was wearing the glasses of codependency. These glasses distorted reality and caused her to interpret life incorrectly. She thought that she was responsible for making her mother happy. When she failed, she felt guilty.

Reasons for a Lack of Objectivity

Why are codependents unable to see reality clearly? Why do they lack objectivity? There are basically two reasons. First, they have an impaired ability to compare reality with unreality. If the environment of their families has been steeped in deception and denial, then they, too, will probably be deceived and lack objectivity. Children believe their parents are god-like. Therefore, they conclude that however their parents treat them is how life really is. If their parents are loving, they surmise that they are lovable. If, however, their parents are manipulative, condemning, or neglectful, they usually conclude that it is somehow their own fault, not their parents'. They see themselves as unlovable and unworthy of love and attention, but they still believe that their parents are always good and right. It is a convoluted, distorted, and tragic perspective. Similarly, marrying or establishing any strong relationship with a person who has a compulsive disorder can slowly erode a person's objectivity. The dysfunctional person lives a lie and expects you to live it, too!

The second reason why codependents lack objectivity is that they fear reality. Solving other people's crises takes so much of the codependent's energy that the prospect of any more pain or anger is simply too much to bear. The fleeting glimpses of reality are so painful that he is afraid of being overwhelmed by it in his own life. This perception is at least partially true. Objectivity does often bring great pain and anger. At times, it can seem truly overwhelming. But reality, with its hurt and anger, is absolutely necessary for healing to occur. Crawling inside an emotional turtle shell may provide temporary relief, but it ultimately brings more long-term pain and prevents the process of healing.

A part of this fear of reality is the fear of losing one's identity. However broken and painful a codependent's self-concept may be, it is all that he has! The fear of losing that morsel of identity is very threatening. Strangely, that leaves him clinging to a dysfunctional person who brings him pain, abuse, and neglect, instead of turning to reality, going through the healing process, and experiencing love, freedom, and strength. The term *denial*, or lack of objectivity, may sound fairly benign, but it is powerful and insidious.

The Periscope and the Wall

Some who are reading this may well say, "I must not have this problem. My friends say that I'm very perceptive." That may be true. Many codependents are among the most perceptive people in the world, but they usually are perceptive about other people, not themselves. One friend of mine can pick up the "vibes" of other people incredibly well and almost read their minds, but he has a very difficult time seeing the effects of his own painful past. For these people, perception is a defense mechanism. In order to please people and gain their approval, they have learned to perceive exactly what they need to say and do. Although they are able to "read" others very well, they can't see that they have lost their own identity and have become virtual puppets, dancing on the strings of those whom they want to please. A codependent who is perceptive about others, but not about himself, is like a man looking through the periscope of a submarine. He can clearly see the waves, the sky, and the ships around him, but he can't see himself or what's going on in the sub. He may be hit by depth charges from destroyers, but he can't see the damage because he's still looking through the periscope. (And a submarine, like codependency, is designed to take you down!)

Other codependents have a different defense mechanism. Instead of developing a finely tuned sense of perception so that they can read people and act in a way that will win approval, they go to the opposite extreme and erect an emotional wall around themselves to block out their pain. They exist in a kind of emotional racquetball court, surrounded by walls, unable to realize how their actions and words are perceived by others, or how they affect others. Erecting these walls may block some of the painful emotions of hurt and rejection, but it also prevents people from experiencing many pleasant emotions like love, warmth, intimacy, and joy. Walls are not selective in the emotions they block.

Black or White

Codependents tend to see life in black or white, seldom in shades of gray. People and circumstances are perceived as being either wonderful or awful. One friend described a coworker to me a few months ago: "He's doing a fantastic job! He is really mature and a hard worker. I'm so glad to be working with him!" But later, the coworker had fallen from grace. My friend excoriated him: "I can't believe what a jerk he is! He has screwed up everything he's touched!" I wondered, *Is this the same person he told me about a couple of months ago?*

I've realized that I do the same thing. I made one of several presentations to a group of executives recently. Afterward, we discussed its merit. As the interaction began, I thought that I had made the better presentation. My ideas were *much* better than those presented by the others. Theirs lacked insight. They lacked courage. They lacked the promise of success. But *my* ideas were brilliant (of course). However, as the interaction continued, I could see that these other people showed a keen understanding of the situation, a clear grasp of others' needs and abilities, and were virtually certain of success. I started to get angry and defend my proposal against their attack.

Then I sat back and thought, *Wait a minute! Their ideas aren't that bad. And mine aren't all that good, either. In fact, they may even be right!* A little objectivity can help us overcome that divisive black-or-white perspective.

A codependent often exaggerates. Making people or situations a little worse than they really are (i.e., black) gives him a sense of identity, of importance. It causes others to be more concerned for him than they might be if he was more objective. Similarly, making people or situations a little better than they really are (i.e., white) makes him look better and more impressive. This is the codependent's goal in relationships: to impress people and/or to get them to feel sorry for him.

An objective person is more balanced because he sees life's good and bad at the same time. He realizes that these exist in tension with each other. A codependent, however, gives up one to embrace the other, which leads to an extreme black-or-white perspective. This exaggerated perception of life causes wide emotional swings, sometimes very quickly and sometimes when the codependent's situation hasn't changed at all!

This chart shows how a codependent's perceptions may differ from an objective appraisal of the same situation:

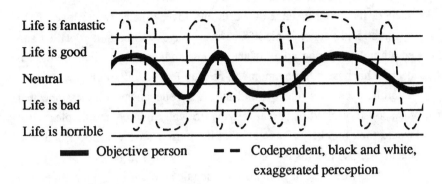

Situations and people are seldom as wonderful or as bleak as the codependent thinks they are.

Not only do codependents distort the truth, they are also apt to believe the distortions of others. How often has a codependent spouse or child heard the words, "I'll never drink again," and believed them, only to watch the alcoholic drink again, and promise again, and drink again, and.... Codependents want so badly to believe that something will be good and right and true that they may completely deny obvious patterns in another person's life, and grab hold of a grand pronouncemen as fact. *Everything will be great now!* they assume, only to be disappointed—again. When the dysfunctional person (or anybody) fails, the promise of hope evaporates into bitterness. The codependent quickly goes from white to black. Somehow, he never thinks to look at the deeds instead of just at the words. He wants so much to believe the best that he denies reality.

Daydreams

Daydreaming is a reflection of the codependent's black-or-white perspective. These daydreams reflect either the negative thoughts of a worst case scenario, or grand and glorious thoughts of the best possible scenario. A codependent can have fantasies about making millions of dollars, being praised and respected, and having all the things he ever wanted, including a sense of worth and love; especially the love of the dysfunctional person in his life. These images can be quite detailed and emotional, conjuring up all of the dreams and/or self-pity that are hidden deep in his heart. In one moment, he may feel elated. In the next instant, an ambulance may roar by, and the poor codependent may assume that his spouse or child or parent is lying critically injured and helpless. He would then be likely to assume that the reason for the accident is due to his neglect, so that his fear is compounded by intense guilt.

Many of these daydreams will include an escape from the abuse and neglect of the compulsive person in the codependent's life. Often, he or she will daydream of escaping from that painful relationship to a lover who is tender, strong, wise, and comforting. The deep anguish of the codependent may even be reflected in daydreams of killing the one who is hurting him or her so deeply.

Reason has virtually nothing to do with these dreams and fears, but the fantasies reflect the codependent's deep hurt, desire for affirmation, and fear of being hurt again.

Blinders

There are numerous other factors, perceptions, and defense mechanisms that prevent the codependent from seeing the truth. Among them:

Selective Filtering of Information

The codependent's mental "grid" filters out a substantial amount of the truth. For example, when her bulimic sister says, for the umpteenth time, "It's over; I'm never going to binge and purge again," the codependent wants to believe it so badly that she feels great relief and joy even though her sister's record of keeping promises is abysmal. Or, he may hear and see only what he dreads. If a codependent is given a performance review at work, there may be twenty things he has done with excellence and efficiency and one area in which he needs to improve. But he will be heart-broken. His mind will be consumed by the one area that needs some improvement instead of the report of his great work in the vast majority of his job.

Defending the Offender

Instead of honestly feeling the hurt of betrayal and experiencing the anger of being abused or neglected, the codependent will usually defend the offender. *It's not really her fault*, she surmises. *She couldn't help it, and besides, it doesn't bother me when she curses me like that. I'm used to it by now.* Or, *Yes, it hurts when he treats me that way, but I feel so sorry for him. He wants to stop drinking, but he just can't.*

Redefining the Pain

Being objective about their deep hurt and seething anger may be painful and/or guilt-inducing for codependents, but repressing these emotions often causes psychosomatic illnesses. Many people who experience the tremendous stress of pain, anger, and guilt develop severe tension headaches, but instead of admitting to their stress, they say that they are having "migraine headaches." One man told me about his "migraines." When I asked him to describe the pain, his description was not of a one-sided, light-sensitive, throbbing pain at all. It was tension, but calling it a migraine shifted and redefined the pain to make it less threatening. A tension headache means he has stress to deal with. A migraine is a vascular problem—no culpability there! A host of other labels are given to ailments that shift the source of the problem from repressed emotions to a purely physical cause. (This, of course, does not mean that every sickness experienced by a codependent is caused entirely by repressed emotions. Buried emotions do, however, lower our resistance to all kinds of physical problems.)

Pronouncements of Perception

A codependent will often make pronouncements of his acute understanding of life's situations, even though he may not see them clearly at all. It's as if his proclamations somehow make his perceptions accurate. He may say, "Oh yes, I see it all now!" Or she may proclaim, "I don't need his love and acceptance. It's never bothered me that he doesn't care about me." These kinds of statements are both the result of poor perception and the means for further denial in the future. If a person feels like his perception is accurate when it's not, then that inaccuracy acts as a defense mechanism which prevents him from seeing reality and feeling pain.

Peer Pressure

The intense peer pressure that adolescents face is difficult for even the most stable teenager to cope with. The added pressure felt by a codependent teenager is indeed intense. Dealing with both peer pressure and objective reality is a double whammy! It is almost as difficult for young adults who experience the peer pressure of entering the "real world" after high school or college.

Too often, objectivity doesn't come until a codependent is in his thirties, forties, or fifties, and the formative, wonderful years of youth have been wasted in the oppressive combination of peer pressure, denial, rescuing, guilt, and pain.

Diversions

All kinds of activities are used by codependents to keep themselves so busy that they don't have time to reflect and feel. Working seventy to eighty hours a week, participating in clubs or sports, watching television, and many other diversions keep them preoccupied. I've heard it said that "activities are often the anaesthetic to deaden the pain of an empty life." Most codependents are unaware that the reason their lives seem empty is because they hurt. They may have a vague, diffuse sense that something is wrong, but they have no idea what it is, and reject any suggestion that they may be dealing with repressed emotions.

Exchanged Emotions

Because codependents haven't experienced very much true love and intimacy or genuine support and encouragement, they often substitute one emotion for another. For instance, one woman (the wife of an alcoholic) equated worry with love. She always seemed to be *worrying* about her son, but she very seldom expressed genuine affection for him. She had substituted the intensity of her worry for the love that he actually needed. Some may use condemnation and praise to manipulate others rather than simply loving them, and some may substitute anger with a stoic calm that has the appearance of peacefulness, but which, in reality, is denial.

Euphemisms

To avoid objectivity about their emotions, codependents often use words that don't accurately reflect how they really feel. The classic example of this is the use of *frustrated* instead of *angry*. People seem to think that it's okay to be frustrated with someone, but real anger is a different story. Real anger is too threatening to the codependent, so he alters his words to make his emotions seem less severe. Though the word *frustrated* is a perfectly legitimate word to describe a mildly negative emotion, it is much overused. In our office, we have agreed not to use the word frustrated, and to go ahead and say that we are angry. People found this to be difficult at first, but after a few days, the honesty was very refreshing!

The "glasses" worn by a codependent distort the truth and obstructs his view of reality. The next several chapters will help you see the effects of codependency more clearly. Objectivity is a most important first step and the beginning of healing.

Questions

1. What are some ways by which you can tell if a person perceives life in the extremes of black and white? Name the words, attitudes, and actions he or she might use:

2. Which of these do you see in your own life?

3. Do you tend to be more extreme (black or white) around certain people or in certain situations? If so, with whom and when?

4. *a*) Describe several of your daydreams:

b) What are their common themes?

5. Examine each of the "blinders" described previously in this chapter. To what degree do each of these block your perception of reality and enable you to avoid pain?

Selective filtering of information

Never   0   1   2   3   4   5   6   7   8   9   10   Always

Defending the offender

Never   0   1   2   3   4   5   6   7   8   9   10   Always

Redefining pain

Never   0   1   2   3   4   5   6   7   8   9   10   Always

Pronouncements of perception

Never   0   1   2   3   4   5   6   7   8   9   10   Always

Peer pressure

Never   0   1   2   3   4   5   6   7   8   9   10   Always

Diversions

Never   0   1   2   3   4   5   6   7   8   9   10   Always

Exchanged emotions

Never   0   1   2   3   4   5   6   7   8   9   10   Always

Euphemisms

Never   0   1   2   3   4   5   6   7   8   9   10   Always

6. How would increased objectivity affect your life?

7. Name several ways and several people that can help you to be more objective. Be specific:

Four

A Warped Sense of Responsibility

A psychiatrist at the Duke University hospital once told me that in a dysfunctional family, one child may become quite irresponsible while another may have an overdeveloped sense of responsibility. This contrast is a typical phenomenon. In one family, a father who was from a military background tried to run his household like a boot camp. There were many demands, a rigid set of expectations, and accolades only for the most exemplary behavior. His wife toed the line as best she could, but soon lost all confidence in her own abilities and opinions. She lost her identity.

Their daughter, Susan, made straight A's through high school. (Anything less would have been intolerable.) She was, for the most part, a very compliant child. But when she went to college, the artificial constraints of her father were no longer there to keep her in check, and Susan began to do virtually all of the things her father detested. She smoked, she drank, she experimented with drugs (and liked them!), she hopped from bed to bed. She had imagined that these things would bring her great freedom and pleasure, but they mostly brought confusion. Her father was kept in the dark about most of Susan's activities, but he knew she was spending more money than he had planned, and that her grades were not what he had expected. And he was furious. At Thanksgiving (their first face-to-face encounter since she had left for college), he exploded at her, but to his shock, Susan exploded right back! During the next three-and-a-half years, their relationship was a blend of an armed truce (those were the good times) and a guerrilla war of subterfuge and sniping.

After graduation, Susan had little to do with her family. She'd bring her new husband and her own growing family for visits, but they were perfunctory, required visits. *Don't call me, I'll call you* was her basic attitude. When her parents needed help, they called on Rob, Susan's younger brother.

Rob grew up in the same environment, but his response in college and after graduation was entirely different. He always tried to please his parents. His mother was appreciative, but his father always expected more. So Rob tried to do more, to be more, to give more, to help more. Everything about his life was characterized by his desire to please his demanding father. Even when he got married, his attention was more focused on his parents than on his wife. His excessive devotion to his parents' desires caused quite a strain in his marriage and in all of his relationships. No matter how hard he tried (and Rob tried very hard!), he couldn't do enough to please everyone, especially his father.

Both irresponsibility and over-responsibility are characteristics of codependency. Both begin with the crushing burden of taking care of dysfunctional people and making them happy. One ultimately gives up. The other keeps trying.

Codependents to the Rescue!

Ray, Diana, Joyce, and I were talking with several others about our deep sense of responsibility for people.

Diana said, "If only I hadn't had to take Christopher to the doctor last week, I could have kept those professors from being kidnapped in Lebanon."

"Yeah, and it was all my fault that the hurricane hit Houston," mused Ray.

Someone else remarked, "I've *got* to do something about the budget deficit." And we all laughed. We were being facetious—sort of. Each of us had felt responsible for solving the world's problems, fixing people's predicaments, and generally making everybody, that is, *everybody*, happy. We were just stating our feelings in their logical extreme.

As we have seen, a codependent often feels unloved. He usually feels that he doesn't have worth or value. How, then, can he gain the value, love, and respect that he so desperately wants? By helping others. When he or she helps somebody, it produces a temporary high: *I'm somebody. I'm appreciated. I have value.* The other person, especially the dysfunctional person, cooperates nicely, thank you, and is glad for the codependent to solve his problems and rescue him. It becomes a treadmill of endless problems and a desperate problem-solver; a needy person and a rescuer.

For the codependent, taking care of others becomes a consuming lifestyle. In his role as caretaker, he is like the man looking through the periscope of the submarine; he doesn't see *his* need to have his own identity, his own dreams, his own emotions, and his own schedule. He is driven to be and do and feel what other people want him to be and do and feel. He believes that doing anything for himself is "selfish."

It has been said that a codependent person can't say no, but that isn't true. He can say no, but when he does, he feels terribly guilty for "being so selfish."

The codependent—the rescuer—lacks objectivity about what the dependent person really needs. He doesn't always need to be rescued! He may need to be left alone. He may need to learn how to be responsible for himself.

Dysfunctional people need to learn to solve their own problems They don't need to be rescued all the time. Rescuing only perpetuates their problems instead of solving them.

Rescuing is an attempt to meet the codependent's need for identity. Our need is to be needed, so we inadvertently make problems worse by looking for every need we can meet. In the process, we make little needs into big ones so we will feel more significant. We read every facial expression and tone of voice so we can say or do just the right thing to make someone else happy. Then, when we have rescued them, we feel great—for a while. If we fail, we feel miserable because the very basis of our self-worth has been shaken.

The emotions of a codependent are dependent on the responses of other people. For instance:

- *If he is angry, it must be my fault. I feel guilty.*
- *If she is sad, I must have done something to hurt her feelings.*
- *If she is afraid, I need to comfort and protect her.*
- *If he is happy, I must have helped him!*

Also:

- *If I am angry, he needs to change how he treats me.*
- *If I am sad, it's her fault.*
- *If I am afraid, he needs to protect me.*
- *If I am happy, it is because she appreciates me.*

In addition to assuming the responsibility of making others happy, codependents expect others to make *them* happy. Personal responsibility (i.e., each person being responsible for himself) is out!

When a child in a dysfunctional family takes responsibility for his parents' happiness, he effectually becomes a parent to his parents. Instead of their nurturing, protecting, and providing for him, he becomes responsible to nurture, protect, and provide for his parents. Roles are reversed: the parents are needy and the child is forced to assume adult responsibilities. He isn't allowed to go through a normal, healthy process of developing his self-concept and identity. He learns to deny his childish emotions and thus stops his development. The resulting damage is deep and prolonged. When children who have "parented" their parents actually become parents themselves, they often expect their children to "parent" them, and the cycle continues.

The codependent's desire to make people happy extends far beyond his own family. He feels responsible for making *everybody* happy. I used to be what salesmen call "an easy mark." I'm quite sure that all the door-to-door salesmen in Texas held a convention and marked our house with a big red pin. They would tell each other, "This guy will buy *anything*: car wash solution, magazines, Girl Scout cookies, oranges, ...*anything!*"

I remember one man who came to our door a few years ago selling a "wonder cleaning fluid."

"It's only $35.00 a gallon, and you would really be helping me out (*the magic words!*) if you would buy some." (He *did* have a slightly pitiful expression.)

Now, who would buy something like this? Who would buy something he doesn't need from somebody he doesn't know at an exorbitant price just to make somebody feel better? That would be ridiculous, wouldn't it? (I've still got about half a bottle left if you want to try it.)

When a codependent helps someone, he feels great, but when he fails, he feels like he has betrayed the other person. These two extremes form a consistent pattern in his life.

The Savior Complex/The Judas Complex

Linda explained to me how she feels responsible for her parents, her husband, her friends, her job, and everything else she touches. She said, "I feel like I need to solve everybody's problems. Nobody else will do it if I don't."

A striking parallel hit me, "You feel like a savior, don't you?" I asked.

Her eyes lit up, then she smiled. "Yes, I do. I guess I'm taking somebody else's role." She laughed at her insight.

A codependent feels like he is either a savior or a Judas; one who rescues or one who betrays, one who helps or one who fails to help. Often, these black-and-white perceptions of himself change in a heartbeat, depending on whether the other person is happy or angry with him.

Michael's father is an alcoholic. His mother would often say to him, "I know I can count on you when I need help." Michael spent his life helping his father stop drinking and helping his mother to help his father stop drinking. "We need to help your father quit," she would say. On numerous occasions, Michael's father would stop drinking for a while. Michael and his mother would be almost euphoric. But then, after a few days, or a few weeks, or a few months, his father's boss would call to say that he had binged at lunch. "Somebody come pick him up, and tell him this is his last day here. I've had it with him!"

How did Michael feel when his father started drinking again? Was he angry with his father? No, he was angry with himself because he had failed. He had let his father—and his mother—down.

How did his mother respond? Was she angry at her husband for being irresponsible and wrecking their lives? No, she blamed Michael and herself because they had failed. Instead of comforting Michael, listening to his hurts and fears and anger, she accused him and withdrew from him. Michael felt terrible for weeks. The savior had become a Judas.

A codependent in his savior mode can believe that he can do no wrong and rescue everyone who is in need. His creed is:

- *If someone has a need, I'll meet it!*
- *If there's not a need, I'll find one, and then I'll meet it!*
- *If there's a small need, I'll make it a large one. Then I'll feel even better when I meet it!*
- *Even if nobody wants help, I'll help anyway!*
- *Then when I've helped, I'll feel good about myself!*
- His family says, "We *knew* we could count on you."

A person with a savior complex thinks he is indispensable. He believes that whatever he is doing is absolutely the most important thing in the world! Nobody else's role even comes close. But in the Judas mode, the outlook is quite different. The mood is one of failure and despair. One man explained, "I feel like I *have* to rescue people, but I'm so afraid of failing that I'm paralyzed." He lives with tremendous tension and heartache. Paralyzing fear and withdrawal prevent the person with a Judas complex from actively rescuing. Therefore, he may not see himself as a codependent. That analysis is erroneous, however. He desperately wants to rescue others just like a codependent in the savior mode, but he can't. His creed is:

- *People need me, but I can't help them.*
- *Their needs are enormous, and I feel awful that I can't help.*
- *Every time I try to help, I mess up.*
- *No matter what I do, it's wrong.*
- *If I try, I fail. If I don't try, I fail. I am a miserable failure.*
- He believes his family would say, "We *thought* we could count on you, but I guess we can't."

How does a person with a savior complex nosedive into a Judas complex? There are three basic ways:

1. He tries to help, but he fails.
2. He tries to help, but he isn't appreciated.
3. He doesn't even try because he's sure he will fail.

In any of these situations, his response is usually withdrawal, guilt, loneliness, anger, self-condemnation, and hopelessness.

The following charts of the savior and Judas complexes correspond roughly to the aforementioned black-and-white extremes the codependent demonstrates due to his lack of objectivity. The difference is that these charts describe the codependent's extremes in his self-concept, either as a rescuer or a betrayer.

A person who is either very skilled at pleasing people (or who is very young and hasn't experienced enough crushing blows of failure) may be in a chronic savior pattern, and know of only a few times when he has felt like a Judas. Often, someone in this condition sees himself as a very healthy and successful person, not as the person he really is.

Chronic Savior Pattern

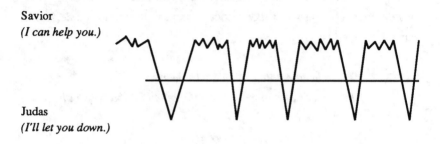

Savior
(I can help you.)

Judas
(I'll let you down.)

A person who has experienced more criticism gradually loses confidence in himself. His chart may look like this:

Mixed Savior/Judas Pattern

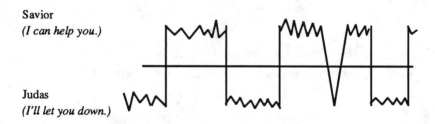

Savior
(I can help you.)

Judas
(I'll let you down.)

Through any number of painful circumstances and through manipulative, condemning people, a person's self-concept may erode to a point where it is characterized almost completely by guilt, despair, anger, loneliness, and hopelessness. This may happen when he is a child, or much later. His life will be characterized by a chronic Judas pattern:

Chronic Judas Pattern

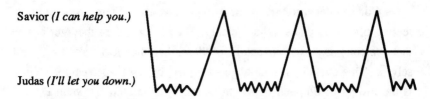

Savior *(I can help you.)*

Judas *(I'll let you down.)*

The savior and Judas complexes are flip sides of the same coin: the need for a sense of worth and the need to be loved and accepted. The savior feels that he is accomplishing that goal. The Judas fears that he can't.

Results of a Warped Sense of Responsibility

Trying to rescue people, or failing to rescue them, results in personal and relational maladies. For example:

Codependents prevent others from developing responsibility

By constantly solving, fixing, helping, and rescuing, codependents deprive others of the opportunity to develop their own sense of responsibility. That keeps them dependent on the codependent, and the cycle continues.

Codependents need to let others do things for themselves!

Codependents neglect themselves

By focusing on others' needs, codependents fail to see their own needs. They derive their self-worth from the opinions of others, using all of their resources to please them. They need their own identity, their own opinions, their own time, their own friends, and their own feelings.

Do things for yourself!

Codependents resent being saviors

Codependents rescue others to feel good about themselves, but this feeling often dissipates rather quickly. They rescue, then they get angry that someone has taken advantage of them, then they feel sorry for themselves. This cycle of rescue-anger-self-pity, or rescue-persecutor-victim is the insight of Stephen B. Karpman and is called the Karpman Drama Triangle.[1]

Codependents threaten, but continue rescuing

When he feels anger and self-pity, a codependent will threaten to stop helping someone, especially another codependent or a person with a compulsive disorder. He says, "That's the limit! That's as far as I go! You have to change your behavior!" But when these threats are consistently followed by more fixing and solving and rescuing, they become meaningless and the one threatened learns he can continue to do as he pleases. He knows he will always be rescued.

Codependents lack objectivity about serving and helping others

Because so much of their lives is spent in helping others, codependents often see themselves as humble (or abused) servants. But there is a great difference between helping people because you want to, and feeling that you have to help others to prevent a loss of value and worth. One is loving service, the other is codependency.

Codependents take themselves too seriously

Several years ago, a coworker told me, "Pat, you take yourself too seriously. Lighten up!"

Fine, I thought, *I'll just give up trying to have a sense of self-worth by accomplishing enough to win the respect and approval of other people. That will help!*

He was right, of course. I was much too serious (and probably still am), but telling me not to take myself seriously doesn't solve the problem. A person's self-worth and value *is* serious, but codependent behavior is not the solution. It is part of the problem.

Questions

1. Define what it means to "rescue" someone:

2. What are some ways you try to rescue others?

3. When do you feel like a savior? How do you act?

4. When do you feel like a Judas? How do you act?

5. How do you feel when you say no?

6. Identify and describe the results of a warped sense of responsibility in your life:

   a) How do you prevent others from developing responsibility? What are the results of your actions?

   b) How do you neglect yourself? Name some results of this behavior:

   c) Are you a resentful savior? If so, how does this affect you and others?

d) Do you ever threaten to stop rescuing, only to continue doing so? Name some results of your actions:

e) Do you seem to lack objectivity about serving and helping others? Describe how this affects you and those you "help" or "serve":

f) If you take yourself too seriously, what are some results of this behavior?

7. How would your life be different if you weren't compelled to help, fix, and rescue? How would your self-concept, your time, your values, and your relationships be affected?

Five

Controlled/Controlling

Without the secure moorings of love, acceptance, and significance, the codependent feels responsible for everything, but confident in nothing. He tries to find his security by pleasing people, by being right, and by doing right things in the right way. His actions are thus like those of a puppet, dancing on the strings of praise and condemnation, easily controlled by the desires of others. Paradoxically, he wants to be in absolute control of his own life so that he won't fail, and he wants to control the behavior of others so that they will add to, and not subtract from, his ability to perform well and please people.

Codependents Are Easily Controlled

Like everyone else, codependents need love and respect, but having been deprived of these precious commodities, they determine to do whatever it takes to win the approval and value they crave. Their means to that end is to make people happy. Their chief fear is that people will be unhappy with them. Those around them quickly learn where the codependent's buttons are and how to push them. Skillful use of praise and condemnation manipulate the codependent as artfully as a marionette manipulates a puppet.

The codependent is pressured to do more and to be more for the other person. He hears statements like:

"95 on an exam isn't good enough."

"I wish you'd get that promotion. I'd be so proud of you!"

"Why do you drive that piece of junk?"

"I'm proud of you for doing so well. I can't wait to tell my friends!"

"You are so wonderful to help me. I wish your sister was as kind as you are."

"You wouldn't be stupid enough to vote for somebody like that, would you?"

"I wish you had come; I really needed you."

"My goodness, what an unusual hair style; I'm sure it will look better when it grows out."

The one who is controlling you probably believes that he is doing you a great favor. He justifies his control over you with statements such as:

"I'm only saying this for your own good...because I love you."

"I know what's best for you. In fact, I know you better than you know yourself."

"I'm your father. If I can't say this to you, who can?"

"If it weren't for me, there's no telling what a mess you'd make of your life!"

These and a myriad of other statements range from severe to delicate manipulation. Each one may, taken alone, sound like a harmless question or statement. But in the context of codependency, where one feels worthless and desperate for love and affirmation, it constitutes an attack designed to change behavior through praise or condemnation. And it works!

Guilt is a primary motivator which usually results in a "have to" mentality. There is no freedom to fail because the perceived risks of losing love and/or respect are too great. Consequently, the codependent is driven. He is obsessive-compulsive. He has to do the right thing, make the clever remark, wear the right clothes, look the right way and, in short, be perfect. (That's not asking too much, is it?) In addition to being driven, he is usually very compliant. He will do anything for anybody at any time with a smile—at least for a while.

Comparison also motivates the codependent. He is compared to other members of the family, coworkers, relatives, and anybody else that might urge him to do more. A friend told me what her mother tells her every month or so: "My friends' children are always doing nice things for them. They buy them clothes, take them on vacations, and buy them jewelry and nice furniture. Their children are there whenever they are needed." But that's not all. "I guess I'll just have to take care of myself." Was that a neutral statement of fact, a statement of independence? No way! She used comparison to manipulate her daughter! Manipulation is not benign. It is evil, seductive, and destructive.

To an objective bystander, the control an abusive person exercises in his family is almost unbelievable. The family, however, is not objective. No matter how much abuse and neglect they endure, their overwhelming thirst for the abuser's acceptance keeps them coming back for more. Charlotte Fedders described the details of her relationship with her abusive husband in her book, *Shattered Dreams*, coauthored by Laura Elliot. Charlotte's husband, John, was both a charmer and a beast. "Like a drug addict, Charlotte would tolerate the deterioration of almost everything else in her life for the rush she felt when John was good to her." [1]

He *was* good to her at times, but he was also physically and psychologically brutal. Right-handed blows to her face, though, didn't hurt as badly as the "black moods" and silences that were triggered by the smallest transgression. Instead of blaming her husband for his selfish and immature behavior, Charlotte blamed herself, and her self-condemnation turned to self-hatred.

Sometimes, John could be charming. He would tell her how beautiful she was, and he would make wonderful promises. Charlotte believed each time that this was it! Now they would be happy! But the dream always died. She lamented, "It's hard to explain how depressed you feel when you realize that things haven't really changed when you thought they were going well. I was so sure that we were making progress, and then John would be moody or silent and we were back to square one. It would make me crazy and so desperate."[2]   Charlotte wasn't able to be objective until later; then, her desperation only made her more easily controlled by John.

Many of us have such little self-confidence that we seldom have our own ideas and desires. We only respond—or react—to the ideas and desires of others. We are like a ball in a pinball machine, being forced in one direction, then another, always doing what the outside force demands, never able to determine its own course.

We learn to react to the slightest hint of praise or condemnation. In fact, we don't even wait for a hint. We anticipate what others might want from us, and act accordingly. We become like puppets on autopilot!

Although the codependent eventually tires of this game, he lacks the objectivity to stop playing. He becomes angry as he realizes that he is being pressured to perform and that he is repeatedly giving in to that pressure. As a result, he hates himself for his foolishness and he hates the dependent person for manipulating him. But because this is the only game he knows, he keeps playing. His desperate need for approval keeps him on the seemingly endless treadmill of need-manipulation-anger. He may even become openly hostile, or more likely, he will become passive-aggressive, refusing to be honest and also refusing to respond. Although he may appear to be passive, his real goal is to hurt the one who has been controlling him.

Any independence demonstrated by the codependent is often tolerated and even encouraged to a certain extent; but beyond that point, it is strictly taboo. Past that point, the dependent person may explode in anger and say, "How could you be so selfish!" or he may take a much more subtle approach: "We need to talk." What he really means is, *We need to talk so I can convince you to go back to being dependent on me, submissive to me, and easily manipulated by me. There should be no limits on what you will do for me. After all, pleasing me is your way of gaining self-worth.*

One woman told me about her relationship with her alcoholic husband. She stated emphatically, "I'm independent now. I don't tell him *anything*!" But her description of their relationship was not one of her growing sense of self-worth. She was simply so hurt that she was withdrawing from him. Her identity and sense of self-confidence weren't any better. She was still "dancing on his strings," doing what he wanted her to do. She simply didn't talk to him as much as she used to, but that wasn't really progress.

Controlling Yourself

Codependents define themselves by what they do, how they look, and how well they accomplish tasks in life. They don't perceive of failure as an option. They have to be right. They have to be in control of their lives. This is because the rest of their life is so chaotic (with a dependent parent or spouse), that they have a strong need to find an area of their lives that can be controlled.

As is usually the case with codependents, there are two extremes: being obsessive-compulsive to gain control of life, or giving up and withdrawing. Some codependents *have* to have order in their lives. Things are in boxes—neatly labeled, of course. The home is tidy, clothes are immaculate, makeup is worn perfectly, every hair is in place, the car is clean (the tank, filled), work is done on time and with excellence. Schedules are meticulously drawn up to aid maximum efficiency and minimize distractions. At best, their sense of satisfaction for doing a job well is very short-lived. It has to be done again tomorrow, and next week, and next month, and....

The obsessive-compulsive wants the people in his life to be in control, too. His spouse, children, coworkers—everybody—needs to contribute to his compelling need for a well-ordered life. Young children often cause the obsessive-compulsive a lot of problems precisely because they are so uncontrollable. When they cry, an obsessive-compulsive can interpret the crying to mean, *There's something wrong. Things are out of control. And it's your fault, Mother* (or *Father*)! Their crying or spilling something—any disruptive behavior—can be a threat to the stability and significance of the obsessive-compulsive because it communicates to him that things are out of control.

The obsessive-compulsive also controls his or her emotions. Not too much crying (maybe none at all), and not too much laughter, either. Anger is expressly forbidden. It means you are really out of control.

The obsessive-compulsive's relationship with God is highly controlled, too. It is often rigid and ritualistic, with good activities, but little spontaneity and warmth.

Of course, no one can be in complete control of his lifestyle, schedule, work, relationships, and emotions all of the time, so obsessive-compulsives are forced to choose which areas they will concentrate on (and get their self-worth from) and which areas to let slide (and say they don't care about).

For some, the crushing weight of being right and neat and in complete control at all times is simply too much. They become immobilized by the perception that the job of controlling life is too massive a task. They appear to be very irresponsible when, in fact, they are obsessive-compulsives who have broken under the strain of striving for perfection. They've given up, but still have no feeling of freedom or relief. Active obsessive-compulsives feel guilty and hopeless, believing that they are terrible failures. One looks very successful. The other doesn't. In reality, both are hurting.

Controlling Others

How the codependent relates to others is usually a mirror of his relationship with the compulsive person in his life. He may hate the way he has been treated, but modeling is a powerful teacher which shapes our patterns of behavior, including how we treat others.

We manipulate others by using the same techniques of praise and condemnation that have been used on us. We use our wit and humor to impress people. Remember, codependents usually have excellent minds and develop strong communication skills to win acceptance. We use sarcasm to cut people to ribbons. ("Just kidding!") And of course, we use praise, anger, and withdrawal to get people to do what we want them to do. These techniques worked on us; they'll work on others most of the time, too.

In our attempt to control people, we usually fall into two extremes again. On the one hand, we may try to "mother" people (in the negative sense of the word), and shape their opinions and habits by constant attention in both praise and criticism. We don't let them out of our sight for long. Or, on the same end of the scale, we may become like dictators, barking orders and exercising our real or perceived authority in their lives. On the other end of the continuum is withdrawal. A person may become so tired of trying to control others, or may feel so inadequate and worthless, that he believes no one will do what he wants them to do. His poor self-concept overcomes his desire to manipulate, and he gives up.

The paradox for the codependent is that while he is trying to control others, he is still being controlled by them. He wants them to perform and appreciate him, but he still gets his self-worth from their approval. One man tried to get his wife, who was addicted to prescription drugs, to pull her act together. Her behavior might cost him a promotion. But she still had him on a string. She could be happy when she wanted, or angry or sad when she chose. That way, she could get him to do almost anything for her. The rabbit was chasing the dog.

We need to take our controls off of other people. We need to let them make their own decisions and live with the consequences. We need to get our self-worth from something other than their approval of us. We need to cut the strings.

Letting people make their own choices can be hard. I give my children, Catherine and Taylor, a small allowance every week. They put it into three boxes: save, spend, and give. Joyce and I tell them that they can use the "spend" money any way they want to. Catherine usually uses her money to buy more lasting toys, like shoe skates. But Taylor has a habit of spending his money (that's a key term in this story: *his* money) on things that he plays with for a day or two and never takes out of the closet again. A few months ago, we went to the store to buy batteries (That's about 742,932 we've bought in the last eight years!), and Taylor spied a toy he wanted. It was a transformable little man in a shark-shaped container. He loves sharks, and he really wanted this toy. I said, "Son, it's *your* choice how you spend your money, but I don't think it's a good idea to spend $9.00 on this. Now, what do you want to do?"

"I like it, Daddy. I'm going to get it."

Round One was lost. Round Two: "Son, you can do whatever you want to. It's your money, but you've gotten other toys like this before. Where are those toys now?"

"I want this one, Daddy." Not a hint of frustration in *his* voice.

Round Three: "Taylor, it's $9.00! You can find something else that you'd enjoy a lot more for that much money. I don't think it's a good idea to get this."

To his credit, he stood his ground. He picked it up and said, "This is the one I want." He took out the wad of dollar bills in his pocket and paid for the toy. He beamed with joy as he walked out of the store.

I quickly realized the error of my ways and apologized. It would have been fine to state my opinion once and give him some helpful advice, but I had gone well beyond that point. I was demanding and was trying to manipulate Taylor, but he was his own man. He made his own choice. Next time, I hope I'll give him the freedom to do that without interfering.

Patterns

In being controlled and controlling others, certain patterns develop in a person's life. Some people are so afraid to be wrong in any given decision that they become passive and indecisive. Others so adamantly feel the need to be right that they state their opinions dogmatically, demanding that others choose to be for them or against them. Between these extremes is mature moderation, the ability to form and articulate opinions without demanding that others agree.

Some of us are on one end of the spectrum about one issue, but on the other end in a different area of our lives. Here's what the continuum looks like:

BELIEFS:	*I'm afraid to be wrong.*	*I have my opinions and you have yours.*	*I have to be right.*
BEHAVIORS:	afraid to state opinions, indecisive, does not trust what he thinks and feels, does not know what he wants	good listener, reflective, decisive without being dogmatic	states opinions dogmatically, opinionated, doesn't listen to others' opinions, demands that others agree with him

I have a friend that I go to lunch with sometimes. When we get together, I ask him, "Well, where do you want to go today?"

He invariably says, "I dunno. Where do you want to go?"

I say, "I don't care. I decided last time. Why don't you decide this time."

After we go back and forth a few times, one of us finally makes a concrete suggestion. What's behind such indecision? It's the fear of making the wrong choice.

On the other end of the spectrum, I know a man who has never (according to his own testimony) been wrong in his life! He always seems to be one step ahead of the rest of us, and always seems to think things through a little more than we do. He is bright, articulate, and persuasive, and when he speaks, he states his opinions as if any sane person would agree with him and only an imbecile would disagree! The people who follow him think he is wonderful. Others are very wary of him, especially if they have been branded as an enemy in one of his black-and-white statements. He forces people to take a stand for him or against him, almost like Colonel Travis drawing a line in the dirt at the Alamo and saying, "If you're with me, cross over this line." (Col. Travis, however, was allowing people to decide if they wanted to try to escape and save their lives. He was giving them an option. He wasn't demanding a response. My codependent friend was demanding the "right" response.)

Why does he act this way? Probably because he is insecure. Though he appears to be one of the most secure people in the universe, he probably feels that he needs strongly defined convictions to designate who he is. And he needs for others to affirm him, so he takes the risk of offending some to win the approval of others.

Codependents desperately need to be loved. They desperately need to *feel* that they are loved and have a sense of worth. When these needs are unmet, some will try to avoid the pain by being indecisive and passive, while others will try to win approval by being right. Most of us are a blend of the two. There are certain people or certain situations which will cause us to withdraw into passivity, but there are other times when we will take a stand, state our opinions forcefully, and hope people like what we've said. Both avenues are designed to get us to the same goal: avoiding pain and winning approval.

Questions

1. Describe three situations in which you felt pressured to perform. Who pressured you? How did he/she pressure you? What would you have lost if you hadn't performed? How did you respond? (Use an additional sheet of paper, if necessary.)

2. How do you feel when you are manipulated and give in?

3. How do you feel when you are manipulated and don't give in?

4. Do you try to control your schedule, your lifestyle, your emotions, etc.? If so, how? What are the results?

5. Describe some ways that people try to control others:

6. How did (does) your family try to control you? In what ways is this like or unlike how you try to control others?

7. What are some situations in which you become passive and indecisive because you are afraid to fail?

8. In what situations do you feel that you have to be right and that people have to agree with you?

Six

Hurt and Anger

Why do some people experience neglect or anger and get over it fairly easily, while codependents react so much more strongly? Or conversely, why do some codependents not react at all?

Abuse comes in many forms. Physical and sexual abuse are not the only kinds. Dr. Susan Forward defined and described how men abuse their wives and lovers. Her definition serves for all other relationships as well. In her book, *Men Who Hate Women and the Women Who Love Them*, she wrote:

> *Abuse is defined as any behavior that is designed to control and subjugate another human being through the use of fear, humiliation, and verbal or physical assaults...[It is] the systematic persecution of one partner by another...they wear down their partners through unrelenting criticism and fault-finding. This type of psychological abuse is particularly insidious because it is often disguised as a way of teaching the woman how to be a better person.* [1]

The results of such abuse are predictable: self-condemnation, morbid introspection, lack of confidence and security, passivity, rigidity, being easily manipulated, and similar emotional and relational maladies.

Active physical and/or verbal abuse in a dysfunctional family leave the codependent feeling deeply hurt and angered by the ones who have hurt him. But the *passive* abuse of neglect and withdrawal are equally devastating. The family that is supposed to provide warmth and worth instead provides pain. The codependent then attempts to please and rescue the one(s) hurting him in order to win the love and approval he so desperately wants. He may even be temporarily rewarded for his attempts to rescue, but this reward will not meet his need for unconditional love, and his hurt and anger will continue to grow. He is trapped in a system which, by withholding love and affection, fuels his compulsion to rescue.

The offenses that a relatively stable person may experience are like a fist hitting an arm. It hurts for a while, but the pain soon disappears. But the same blow to a codependent is more severe. His emotional arm is already broken; so, the pain of being hit is much more overbearing. And it lasts much longer.

Hurt and anger go hand-in-glove. Hurt is the result of not being loved, not being valued. It comes from feeling abandoned, used, and condemned. Anger is the reaction toward the source of the hurt.

These painful emotions are not only products of the codependent's past, they are a part of his reality every day. The need to have a sense of worth leads him to try to rescue the one who has hurt him, but inevitably, he gets hurt again and again. And sooner or later, he gets angry.

Marianne's husband, Kyle, was an alcoholic. Under her pleas and cajoling, he would stop drinking at times, only to slide back eventually into the abyss again. She made excuses for him. She worked to support the family because he couldn't keep a job. She repeatedly explained to their children that "Daddy is sick today. We'll have to be real quiet and get him whatever he needs."

Occasionally, this overwrought woman would reach her limit. She'd had enough! And she'd tell him she wasn't calling in to say he was sick today. He'd have to call himself. (Big threat, huh?) But his response was usually something like, "How can you be so selfish? I'm only asking you to do one little thing for me, and you won't do it. If you loved me, you'd do it for me."

That was low. A codependent lives by rescuing, by helping, by enabling. Calling a codependent "selfish" is the worst thing in the world! Marianne was cut to the quick. She made the call (of course!). Then she realized that he had done it again. He had gotten his way. He had won—no, he had manipulated her into doing what he wanted her to do! She was furious! But not so furious to refuse the option of rescuing him the next time, and the next, and the next, and....

The pain and anger within a codependent's soul are deep and black. Even a glimpse of them can seem overwhelming. Elaborate defense mechanisms are thus erected to block pain and to control anger. These defensive "layers" include a denial of reality, pleasing people, being in control, keeping people at a distance, being numb to feelings, displacing anger, excusing the offender(s), and many other variations. Some of us use different defenses for different circumstances, but most of us have developed several layers to ensure our protection.

By enabling us to block out pain and control our anger to some degree, defense mechanisms bring short-term gain. But they yield long-term losses by preventing us from beginning the healing process. These layers of defense mechanisms need to be peeled away to expose our pain and anger so that these issues can be dealt with.

Objectivity is the first step toward healing. We'll gain more insight about ourselves by examining some common ways that codependents respond to their hurt and anger:

Numbness

I don't want to feel this way, so I won't. This is a personal philosophy for some of us. Our pain is too great, so we block it out. Our anger is too frightening, so we act like it's not there. We are forced to live life at the surface emotionally because what's underneath is simply too much to bear. We have superficial emotions and superficial relationships.

One young lady described her parents. They divorced when she was seven years old. Her father remarried and moved away. Her mother went to work to support her and her brother. Her father sent her gifts for a couple of years after he left, but he later faded from her life. Her mother was frazzled and frantic as an abandoned, working, single parent. "How do you think your parents' divorce has affected you?" I asked.

"Oh, not much at all."

"Do you miss your father?"

"No, not really."

"Do you feel especially close to your mother since she's taking care of you so well?"

"Yeah, I guess so, but we're not that close."

She seemed a bit detached from her situation, so I asked a different question. "What makes you really happy? What do you really enjoy?"

She thought for a minute. "I can't think of anything."

"What makes you really angry? What upsets you?"

"Not much," she replied blankly. "I don't feel much of anything."

Over the next several months we talked more about her past, and she began to feel more. Some of the feelings were painful. Some were pleasant. It was a mixed bag, but she was becoming more in touch with her life and her feelings.

Sometimes, codependents conclude that since feelings are painful, they must be wrong. Although we try to make others happy, we suppress our own feelings. But there's a problem: we can't be picky about which aspects of our emotions we suppress. We can't stifle the bad feelings and enjoy the good ones. When we repress the painful feelings, we quell the enjoyable ones, too.

Some of us hurt so deeply that we believe we are totally worthless. We think we cannot possibly be worthy of someone else's love. One man who had repressed his emotions throughout his life developed some relationships with people who really cared about him. Most of the time, he was numb to their affection and affirmation, but occasionally they got through to him. How did he respond? He wept, and he withdrew from them. He said sadly, "It hurts too much to be loved." Sooner or later, the consistent environment of love and acceptance will chip away the defensive layers this young man has developed, and he will be able to feel the pain of his past as well as the love of the present and the future.

Another way we may try to avoid pain is by staying so busy that we don't have time to reflect. We can stay numb. The theme song for those of us with this tendency is Carly Simon's, "Haven't Got Time for the Pain." When we fill our lives with activities and superficial relationships, we don't have time to feel pain.

Pain Without Gain

Some of us may wish we were numb, but we aren't. We hurt. We hurt so badly we can hardly stand it. There is a feeling of being crushed, hopelessly crushed. An intense feeling of loss with no hope of gain consumes us. We feel as though we've been broken into a million pieces, and there isn't any glue to fix us. No healing; only hurt.

Because we can't go through life admitting this kind of hurt to others, we put up a facade of competence and happiness. Few people ever realize the blackness that lurks beneath the neon outside.

A woman whom most people would describe as healthy and mature came to see me. She said she had to talk to somebody; that she thought she was becoming deranged. Though she has lots of friends and is considered a successful mother, business woman, and church member, she was dying inside.

She described her home life. On the surface it seemed normal enough: no alcoholism, no divorce, no addictions. Yet, she described her parents' relationship as cool and aloof, like an armed truce. Their relationship with each other mirrored their relationship with her. Though there were no outward signs of a dysfunctional family, they were, in fact, quite dysfunctional. She had been left an emotional orphan, fending for herself, lacking the love, protection, and support that every child needs. Like other codependents, she tried to win love by rescuing.

She wept, "My father never held me. He never told me that I was his special little girl or anything. I want to be loved so much, but no matter what I've done to please him, I've never felt that he loves me."

In fact, this dear woman is afraid to be loved. She is afraid that if she experiences someone's affection, it may be taken away from her, and the pain would be unbearable. She wants to be loved so badly; she needs it so desperately, but she's afraid of being hurt even worse than she hurts now. That is hurt with no hope; hurt with no healing.

Many of us live with a continued sense of impending doom. We believe that we don't deserve good things to happen to us. We don't deserve people to love us. When good things do happen, we may then assume that something bad will occur to balance the good. One college student explained to me that he had really enjoyed his vacation at spring break, but that his enjoyment was tempered by the prevailing belief that something very bad would happen as soon as the break was over. That gloomy assumption stole his joy from a delightful situation.

Believing that we are inherently bad people, who are unworthy of love, leads to self-condemnation, and ultimately, to self-hatred. Some of us think and say terrible things about ourselves. We call ourselves horrible, degrading names. If we heard someone saying those same things to another person, we would describe it as hatred and abuse. We don't call it abuse when we call ourselves these names, however, because we believe that we deserve that kind of treatment.

Excusing the Offender/Blaming Ourselves

Often, where there is hurt without healing, there is hurt without anger at the offender. The anger is displaced, but the offender is excused for his offense. The desire to "believe the best" of the one who has hurt us blocks our objectivity. Instead of blaming him, we blame ourselves.

Thomas described his childhood. His father was a workaholic who traveled several days a week and often worked on weekends. Thomas' mother had difficulty coping with her husband's neglect, so she ate to soothe her pain. Because there was a lot of pain, there was a lot of eating. She weighed almost 300 pounds. She tried to love Thomas enough for both herself and his mostly-absent father, but her good intentions led her to smother him. She told him what to wear, where to go, which friends to play with, what to think, and how to feel. Thomas had great difficulty in college and in marriage. He never seemed to have an opinion of his own.

Neglect by one parent and smothering attention by the other do not promote stability, confidence, and maturity.

As Thomas described the details of his life, I asked him, "How do you feel about yourself?"

"Terrible!" he snapped. "I can't do anything right. I don't know how I feel. I don't know what to do."

"How do you feel about your parents?"

"Oh, they did the best they knew how. It's not their fault. If I had been a better son, they wouldn't have had such trouble with me."

"What do you mean: *such trouble*?"

"Well...I just didn't turn out the way they wanted me to. I wish my parents were proud of me, but they're not. It's all my fault."

Thomas' mother internalized her anger and pain, and comforted herself with food. Thomas grew up internalizing his anger and pain, too. He blamed himself for being neglected by his father and for being manipulated by his mother. He excused the offenders and blamed himself.

Displaced Anger

Codependents often express repressed anger at people or things that have nothing to do with its cause. Their anger surfaces at odd times and in odd ways.

Don's disposal broke. The motor hummed, but the carrots stayed in one piece. Being a frugal homeowner, he went to an appliance store and bought a new disposal. When he got home, he rolled up his sleeves, got out his tools, and plunged into the black hole under the sink. The first part of the operation went without a hitch. The old disposal came off easily. But when he tried to put the new one on, Don found that the intake and outlet holes were in different places than on his old one. This called for some creative plumbing!

The tube from the dishwasher to the disposal wasn't quite long enough, but if the disposal could be pushed over just a little, then clamped...there! So what if it slanted to the right a little, the rubber seal at the top would keep it from leaking. But with it leaning that way, the pipe that went out of the bottom on the left wasn't long enough. If the clamp could be put on really tight it would work. Wrench, please. A tug on the pipe to pull it as close as possible, then tighten the clamp...one more turn to make it really tight and...crunch! The pipe split!

Don took his wrench and beat the stuffing out of the pipe! (It wasn't split anymore; it was pulverized!) After a few expletives, he threw his wrench into the tool box and stomped off to buy more pipe.

Now why did Don get mad at that pipe? Did it call him dirty names? Did it say ugly things about his wife, or push his little girl down on the playground? It was simple physics. The pipe is a *thing*. It had no personal vendetta against Don. Why was he so mad?

When he was growing up, Don's father had never been very handy around the house. He always felt like a failure when he tried to do anything mechanical. When Don tried to work on things, his father would often stand nearby and say, "You'll mess it up. You're gonna break it. You can't do it." Hearing that once would be painful, but hearing it often and in every kind of context hurt him deeply. It made Don angry with his father, but he never said anything to him about how he felt. Don wasn't angry at the pipe. He was angry with his father. His anger at the pipe was displaced anger.

Outbursts of Anger

Codependents may not only get angry at the wrong thing or person, they may also become disproportionately angry. Their suppressed anger may explode like a tube of toothpaste that is squeezed until it pops and toothpaste squirts in all directions.

Betty's father was an alcoholic. He occasionally beat his wife and children. As the youngest of six, Betty was terrified of him. The one stabilizing force in the family was her mother, but after years of neglect and abuse, she couldn't take any more punishment. She committed suicide when Betty was twelve.

As a child, Betty was never able to discern the difference between her father's angry threats and her mother's quiet defense of the children; so, when Betty grew up and had her own family, she treated her three children both ways. She wanted to protect them and care for them, but when they disobeyed, she flew into a fury, threatening them with brutal beatings. "I'll whip you with the buckle end of a belt if you do that again!" she would scream. But she seldom followed through on her threats. She wanted to be gentle, yet found herself yelling at her children for even insignificant things. Then she felt deep pangs of guilt.

In another situation, Ken's mother couldn't handle the stress of raising a family, so she vanished when he was six years old, leaving Ken and his brother with their father. He didn't do much better, sending the boys to stay with various aunts and uncles so he wouldn't be bothered by them.

Ken was a likable guy most of the time. In fact, he was very popular, especially with women. His tendency was to begin a deep, absorbing relationship with a girl, only to drop her and find another one. When a friend would ask him why he'd stopped dating a girl, Ken would snarl, "That's none of your business! You don't understand me! Stay out of my life!" (And that was to a friend!)

Ken was a good athlete and he loved to play softball. But he had to win. He had to get hits. He had to make every play on the field. When he made errors or outs, it seemed to flip a switch inside him. He would throw his bat, kick the ground, and curse.

In conversations, Ken always had an opinion...the right opinion. If people disagreed with him, even in the most polite or abstract terms, he would take their comments as a personal offense. In his mind, people were either for him or against him. If you agreed with him, he was your best friend. If you didn't agree, you were his sworn enemy, and he would stiffen and snarl insults.

When things went well, Ken was fine. But when they didn't, his outbursts of anger were lethal.

Using Self-Pity and Anger to Manipulate Others

Hurt and anger are powerful emotions. They affect us deeply and can be used to affect others, too. They can be powerful forces of manipulation to get others to care about us and dance to our tune.

In the previous story, we looked at Ken, a deeply troubled young man who was obviously hurt by his parents' neglect. His seething anger often boiled over. To win the affection (i.e., pity) of others, especially that of sensitive and caring women, Ken would often describe his horrible childhood in detail. His story of painful neglect, occasional abuse, abandonment, and heartache won the hearts of many. He also won their admiration by describing how he now had a grip on life, despite the cards being stacked against him.

When his uncontrolled, violent outbursts of anger threatened to shatter the heroic image he was portraying to others, he would say sadly, "You just don't understand. If you had parents like mine, you wouldn't be nearly as mature and stable as I am." Self-pity usually restored his place of esteem.

But anger was also a means of manipulation for Ken. People became afraid of him early in their relationship with him. A raised eyebrow or a raised tone of voice meant that you were treading on thin ice, and you'd better agree with him—or else! Both violence and the threat of violence were intimidating. Ken got what he wanted: self-pity, respect (or was it only fear?), and acquiescence.

The codependent is the product of manipulation, neglect, and abuse, but he can use these powerful forces on others as well. Not all are so blatant as Ken. Most are more subtle but just as effective in eliciting the responses of pity and fear (poor counterfeits of love and respect) that they really want and need.

Memories

When a person begins to get in touch with the pain of his past, he will often remember events that have long been buried in his mind and heart. The hurt and anger that these memories evoke are painful, and some people may interpret this pain as going backward. But it is progress.

I was riding in my car with Carl, a long-time friend. We were discussing codependency and the events in our lives that had caused us pain. There was a short lull in our conversation; then, Carl groaned.

I wondered what was wrong.

"I just remembered something that I haven't thought of in thirty years," he said.

I waited for his explanation, then he said: "When I was seven years old, my older brother got in a habit of stealing money from me. I told my folks, but I guess they just didn't want to be bothered with it. Anyway, they didn't do anything. I was pretty good with money. I saved my allowance and earned extra money so I could buy kites and baseball cards and stuff like that.

"But my brother wasn't so responsible. He wanted his allowance, my allowance, and any other money I made, so he just took it. After a few weeks of having money mysteriously disappear (I knew where it went, but he would just laugh at me when I accused him.), I realized that I *had* to do something. So I got my Bible and opened it to Exodus 20 and the Ten Commandments. I underlined verse fifteen, *You shall not steal*, and put my money jar next to it.

"I felt really good. Surely *nobody* would steal money from a jar next to a Bible that was open to the commandment not to steal! But you know what? That jerk took my money anyway! I couldn't believe he would do that to me! You know, it makes me mad to think about it now—and that was thirty years ago!"

We rode down the highway. The memory of that offense—his brother stealing from him and laughing about it—was painful, but it was a part of the healing process for Carl.

At the core of a codependent's heart are hurt and anger—results of the abuse, manipulation, and/or neglect experienced in a dysfunctional relationship. We try to obstruct pain and control anger any way we can, but these defense mechanisms are counterproductive. We need objectivity and truth. We need patience to go through the process of pain so that healing can take place. But it's not time for solutions yet. We need more objectivity about our guilt and loneliness.

Questions

1. Why is there so much hurt and anger in a codependent's life?

2. What are some reasons why we try to obstruct pain and control anger?

3. Do you see any of the following in your life? If so, describe in detail...

   a) Numbness:

   b) Pain without gain:

c) Excusing the offender/blaming yourself:

d) Displaced anger:

e) Outbursts of anger:

f) Using self-pity and anger to manipulate others:

4. Are you afraid to face hurt and anger in your life? Why, or why not?

5. Who or what can help you to be honest and express your pain in a safe environment?

Seven

Guilt

Codependents often feel guilty. They feel guilty for what they've done and haven't done. They feel guilty for what they've said, haven't said, felt, and haven't felt. They feel guilty for just about everything. Often such guilt produces feelings of worthlessness and shame.

The codependent gets his worth—his identity—from what he does for other people. He rescues, he helps, he enables, but no matter how much he does for others, it's never enough. That's the trap of living in a dysfunctional family. He rescues, but he is rejected. Lacking objectivity, he concludes: *It's my fault. If I were a better person, they would love me.* So he spends his life trying to be good enough to earn the love and acceptance he so desperately wants, but fears he will never have. And he's haunted by the shame that he hasn't, or can't, measure up.

The guilt and shame that I'm referring to are not the kind that promote an objective judgment of our offense. If you have been caught going 85 mph on the highway, and the judge pronounces, "Guilty as charged," that is objective guilt. In that sense, all mankind stands before God as guilty and in need of the forgiveness and acceptance of the cross. But the guilt that we are looking at in this chapter is a different kind. It lacks objectivity. It is devoid of forgiveness. It is without love and acceptance. It is the painful, gnawing perception that you are worthless, unacceptable, and can never do enough to be acceptable, no matter how hard you try.

There is a vast difference between these two kinds of guilt. One produces a sorrow that leads to positive, refreshing change. The other leads to a sorrow that only crushes. The apostle Paul described positive and negative guilt in his second letter to the Corinthian believers:

I now rejoice, not that you were made sorrowful, but that you were made sorrowful to the point of repentance; for you were made sorrowful according to the will of God, in order that you might not suffer loss in anything through us. For the sorrow that is according to the will of God produces a repentance without regret, leading to salvation; but the sorrow of the world produces death.

2 Cor. 7:9-10

The realization of personal wrong, coupled with a knowledge of forgiveness, brings hope and change, but the realization of personal wrong without that forgiveness brings bitter pangs of condemnation and hopelessness. In dysfunctional families, personal wrongs are magnified while forgiveness, love, and acceptance are withheld. Those bitter pangs of condemnation are a way of life for the codependent.

Guilt Crushes

Guilt crushes a person. It crushes his dreams, his desires, and his personality. If your worth comes only from helping others, then you can't say no to anything or anyone. If you do say no, or even if you say yes and fail (or if you succeed but others don't appreciate you), then your worth is shattered. Even success and praise bring only short-term relief. There is always the nagging fear of losing that approval. To please people, you take on their dreams and desires, not your own, and lose your personality in the process.

All of us have done things that are wrong, but a codependent attaches greater weight to those wrongs than he does to forgiveness. He is deeply ashamed, feeling that at least some of those terrible things he has done cannot possibly be forgiven.

One man described his constant pangs of guilt in a small group setting. When someone asked, "Harry, when are you happy? When do you feel good?" he replied with a forlorn expression, "I don't want to be happy. I'm not a good person, so I don't have any right to feel good." Harry was tolerant of his parents' neglect (too tolerant, due to his lack of objectivity), but he was totally intolerant of the slightest mistakes, or even the perceived mistakes, of his own.

Rescuing is seen as life's greatest good by the codependent. Selfishness is the worst sin. After all, his very identity comes from being unselfish and giving until it hurts (no, far beyond where it hurts!). The accusation of selfishness is indeed a severe condemnation that threatens his only foundation: his ability to help others. This fact is not lost on the dysfunctional family. The quickest way to get a codependent person to cower and give in is to pull out the *big gun*: "You're so selfish! How can you even think of not doing what I ask you to do?" This confirms his worthlessness and "pulls his strings."

Anger compounds the guilt and reinforces the codependent's tragic sense of worthlessness. One friend of mine explained how he was pushed to the limit to help his wife, who had an eating disorder. He got very angry. But then he thought, *She can't help it. If I were the kind of husband she needed, she'd be okay. It's all my fault!* He was infuriated again, but this time, at himself for getting angry with his "poor, helpless" wife. He cursed himself, and called himself degrading and vile names. He even considered punishing himself for being so selfish and callous.

The crushing effects of guilt, shame, worthlessness, self-hatred, and self-condemnation take a heavy toll. Some people escape into a shell of numbness, passivity, or depression. Some develop psychosomatic illnesses. And some just plod along, day after day, year after year, under the oppressive weight of guilt. There are varieties of results, but one cause: the crushing nature of guilt.

Guilt Motivates

The only way to win at life, the guilt-ridden codependent surmises, is to earn the respect of others. Lacking objectivity, that's his only choice. He feels worthless; he feels unloved, and he concludes that there must be something wrong with him. He then feels guilty. And he is thus compelled to take action which, he hopes, will make up for his shortcomings.

The hope of gaining acceptance and the threat of losing it are powerful motivators. They prompt the codependent to rescue people who take advantage of him. They motivate him to help people who don't appreciate him. Oh, he gets a little of what he craves; some appreciation and respect. He gets just enough to keep him on the hook, but not enough to really satisfy him. So he keeps running on the endless treadmill of hope, guilt, and fear.

Motivation by guilt is usually associated with the desire to avoid condemnation and the desire to perform, or measure up to standards set by someone else or ourselves. We perform with a sense of urgency and desperation because we think we *have* to, not because we *want* to. Our motivation is characterized by *I have to* and *I can't* statements:

> *I have to accomplish this or that task today.*
> *I have to go here.*
> *I have to help this person in this way at this time.*
> *I have to say yes.*
> *I have to control my anger and hurt.*
> *I can't fail in this assignment.*
> *I can't let her down.*
> *I can't let my anger get out of control.*
> *I can't say no.*

Statements like these are the creed of the obsessive-compulsive codependent. They are the painful taunts of dismal failure to the one who has given up and withdrawn into passivity. Either way, they form the warp and woof of the codependent's mental fabric. There is no need to give illustrations at this point, because virtually every illustration in this section of the book is one of guilt motivation.

The capacity to say no, to make our own decisions, to relax, and to enjoy life are foreign to us because they don't contribute to our consuming goal in life: the acquisition of worth.

Guilt motivation can be a more subtle, but just as painful, form of manipulation. It is not only the desire to avoid condemnation, but also the need to win love and affection. Susan, for example, grew up in a dysfunctional family. Her mother was an alcoholic. Her father was passive. She knew something was wrong, and she concluded that whatever it might be was somehow her fault. She desperately wanted to be loved, and when she was eight or nine years old, she often saved enough money to buy gifts for her family. She got on her bike and pedaled to town. There, she spent her hard-earned money to buy tobacco for her father, a cheap necklace or handkerchief for her mother, and a toy for her sister. She would ride back home with great hope in her heart and present these gifts at supper. Her father, mother, and sister politely said "Thanks," but after she went to sleep one night, her mother asked her father, "I wonder why Susan keeps buying us these silly little things. Why do you think she wastes her money like that?" She had no idea that little Susan was trying to buy love.

Codependents live by *should's* and *ought's* not by the confidence of security and significance. They are driven to have more, to be more, to say more, and to do more. The carrot dangles from the stick, always just out of reach. No matter how much he does, no matter how much he has, no matter how clever or successful he is, the codependent almost always has the nagging thought that *I should have done more, I ought to have said something else*, or *I should have been better*.

Glenn tried everything to please his demanding wife. He worked long hours to provide extra money so she could have nicer clothes and furniture. He kept the yard immaculate. She told him, "You ought to trim that bush more often. What will the neighbors say?"

"Okay, honey," was his passive reply.

He brought her breakfast in bed almost everyday. In spite of this, she seemed to have a mental list of everything every husband had done for his wife since the beginning of time, and she expected Glenn to do them all. In short, he was her slave. He was a slave to her ought's and should's.

In businesses, churches, and community organizations, codependents usually equate their guilt-motivated drive with commitment. They have intensity to accomplish goals, but with what purpose? Often, it is to earn the respect they want and to avoid rejection. In business, they dread hearing performance standards and personnel reviews because they fear that they may not meet the requirements.

Is this wrongly-motivated drive the fault of the codependent, his boss or, in a church, his pastor? Did the codependent interpret normal life through his own distorted guilt filter and deduce that the system is at fault? Or does the boss or pastor induce guilt motivation by a manipulative use of praise and condemnation? These are not easy questions to answer. It could be on one side or the other, or it could be both. If a large group of people fear failure and rejection, then the system itself is probably guilt inducing. It is a curious fact, however, that guilt motivated people are attracted to the rigidity and demanding environment of guilt-producing organizations. They feel more comfortable with rules, formulas, high expectations, and should's and ought's. They may not feel loved there, but at least they know where they stand in required behaviors and activities. For the same reason, a daughter of an abusive alcoholic father often falls into a pattern of marrying and divorcing abusive, alcoholic husbands. That's the only kind of relationship she knows.

Some codependents, who are crushed by guilt and have retreated to passivity, are poor workers. But most of us are the best workers businesses and churches have because the stakes are so high: we have to avoid condemnation and gain a sense of worth. (I am not saying that a person who overcomes his codependent lifestyle will be a lazy slob.

Secure, stable people are usually hard-working people, but they work hard for a different reason: to help others, not to gain a sense of worth.)

Introspection

A codependent either tries to stifle pain by putting up a wall and refusing to think about life, or by thinking about himself. All day. Everyday. In this introspective mode, he analyzes his every word, conversation, action, and thought. This seems paradoxical: he devotes his life to rescuing and helping others, but he thinks about himself all the time. But remember his reasons for rescuing and helping: to gain a sense of worth, to be loved, and to gain the respect and appreciation that he so desperately wants.

There is a great difference between reflection and morbid introspection. Reflection is based on reality. It is objective, healthy, and not predisposed to condemnation. Morbid introspection is quite different. An introspective person digs through his thoughts and motives and actions with twin hopes: to find the wrong in his life so he can change it, and to find right in his life so he can feel good about himself. But this incessant digging is not objective. It does not begin with a sense of value and worth. On the contrary, it begins and continues with the underlying pessimistic assumption: *there's something very wrong with me, and I've got to make it right.* With that assumption, self-condemnation dominates his thinking, but since feeling hurt and anger are not permitted (they are considered "wrong"), these painful feelings are internalized and the downward spiral continues.

In a relationship with a pathological, compulsive person, the introspective codependent tries to rescue and enable, and then feels angry because he has been used. In his blindness, however, he justifies the behavior of the compulsive person and blames himself in vehement terms for being so selfish that he would get angry with such a "poor sick person."

How could you? he asks himself if no one else asks him. *How could you be so selfish and cold-hearted? Don't you know that your poor father* (or mother or sister or brother or...) *is sick? Is that the kind of compassion you have in your heart, that you'd get mad at a sick person who can't help it?* The crescendo builds. *What's wrong with you?*

This kind of self-condemning introspection is usually followed by epithets, expletives, and vicious name-calling—all directed at himself. Then, a period of days or weeks of penance—feeling bad enough for long enough—is designed to pay for his sin of selfishness. The problem with this method—aside from theological reasoning—is that there usually arises another situation, similar to the one preceding it, before penance is completed for the first alleged offense. The introspective person then finds himself doing penance for several offenses at the same time and the load becomes oppressive indeed.

Morbid introspection is not confined to relationships with compulsive people. It is only at its worst there. It permeates every facet of the codependent's life, so that he analyzes everything and everyone to the "nth" degree, hoping to ferret out the wrongs in his life and find something (anything!) good so he can have a sense of worth. This is consuming. It is deadly. It will eat your lunch.

Comparison

One of the prime ingredients of introspection is comparison. A person who lacks security and significance needs some means of determining where he stands. Comparison is the perfect solution! He needs to be one step further, one notch higher, one quip wittier, a bit better looking than other people.

If the codependent can't think of enough standards to compare himself to, his dysfunctional relatives will usually help him. They will compare his clothes, his hair, his job, his children, his intellect, his athletic ability...as if he needs any help!

This comparison feeds the fantasies of the introspective codependent. He imagines himself getting accolades and promotions, having beautiful things, and accomplishing great feats of daring...all just a little bigger and better than someone else.

Guilt Makes You Crazy

Deep within our minds and hearts, we sometimes ask ourselves, *What's wrong with me? Am I crazy?* Life is so hard. Even the fun things—things that we hope and dream will bring satisfaction and relief—even those things turn out to be hard. The people who are supposed to be supportive and affirming often turn out to be critical and aloof. Were they like that already, or did we somehow make them that way? Why is *everything* so hard?

A squeeze-play is at work here. On one side, pressing against you, are all the desires and hopes and dreams of asserting yourself, being creative, and having a sense of worth. On the other side is guilt for being so selfish in wanting those things. In the middle, these forces squeeze out your vitality and confidence, leaving you with feelings of confusion and self-condemnation.

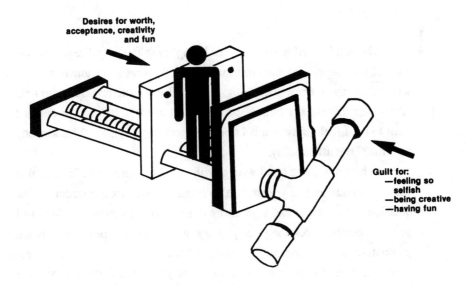

Desires for worth, acceptance, creativity and fun

Guilt for:
—feeling so selfish
—being creative
—having fun

Jenny expressed to me her desire to do some creative things for Christmas. She wanted to decorate the house, fix special presents, bake, and in general, make the holiday a meaningful, festive, and colorful season. "But these things take so much time," she lamented. "And I could probably use my time more effectively doing other things."

"Like what?" I asked.

"Oh, I don't know. Like helping out at church, or doing things for my neighbors, or cleaning the garage. It's a mess."

It seemed that she had an almost endless list of "good things" to do, but she didn't want to do those. She wanted to do something else, but she felt guilty for even considering it. "I'm so selfish," she concluded.

Then she went through a list of questions to help her analyze her predicament:

> *How can I get more done?*
> *Which of my desires are okay and which aren't?*
> *What is the wise thing to do?*
> *What is most productive?*
> *Why do I feel so guilty when I want to do something creative and fun?*

She condemned herself for not living up to perceived expectations, and yet was angry that she might not get to do what she wanted to. Her sense of always *having* to do things that appeared more productive to help others was driving her into despair and confusion. "If I do the things I want to do, I feel guilty, but if I don't do them, I get angry. What's wrong with me?" she asked sadly.

"There's nothing at all wrong with you," I assured her, "except that you won't relax and be yourself. You're asking the wrong questions. The question is not, 'How can I get more done?' The question is, 'How do I get my worth?' As long as you try to get your worth from being productive and incessantly serving others, you will feel pressured, condemned, and confused for having any desires and dreams of your own. But you already have worth! You already have value! You can be yourself. Everything you do doesn't have to be productive. You don't have to serve others all the time. As you express yourself and gain a sense of confidence, you'll feel the freedom to be yourself more often. And you'll do things that are productive and helpful for others, but you'll do them because you *want* to, not because you think you *have* to."

One conversation won't change the years of repressed desires and guilt motivation that have squeezed the life out of Jenny and made her feel that she was going crazy. But it's a start.

Using Guilt on Others

The law of sowing and reaping takes effect in the area of guilt just as it does in every other part of life. Like begets like, and if guilt has been used to motivate and manipulate you, you will probably use it on others. It is a strange fact that even if you detest the way you have been treated, that model is so strong that you may find yourself treating others the same way.

A father realized that he both condemned his children and withdrew his affection from them to manipulate their obedience. He felt terrible about it. He loathed and despised himself when he did it, but this was how his parents had treated him. It was the only way he knew to do, even though he realized it was wrong and knew how much it had hurt him.

The same words of praise and condemnation; the same actions, tone of voice, and expressions; the same aggressive, angry behavior; and the same withdrawal and passivity that are used to manipulate us are the ingredients we tend to use with others. Or, on the other end of the spectrum, instead of harshly condemning, we withdraw; instead of being passive and neglectful, we smother. A poor model will produce a poor offspring. He may be a duplicate or an opposite, but he will be out of balance either way.

Guilt is a way of life for the codependent. The nagging pain of believing, *There's something wrong with me, and I've got to fix it,* is a powerful and destructive force. We need to see this for what it is: evil and destructive.

Questions

1. Explain why codependents so often feel guilty:

2. What are some of the differences between *the sorrow that produces a repentance without regret* and *the sorrow that produces death?*

3. Do you see any of the following aspects of guilt in your life? If so, describe how these affect your self-concept and your relationships.

   a) Guilt crushes:

b) Guilt motivates:

c) Introspection:

d) Comparison:

e) Guilt makes you crazy:

f) Using guilt on others:

4. What would your life be like if you had a strong sense of worth and were not plagued by guilt?

Eight

Loneliness

Codependents spend their lives giving, helping, and serving others. From the outside, they may appear to be the most social people in the world, but inside they are lonely. Their attempts to please others by helping and serving are designed to win affection. Though they may occasionally see a glimpse of love and respect, it usually fades all too quickly. Then, thinking they have been abandoned by both people and God, they feel empty and companionless. They distrust authority, believing that anyone above them is against them, and they build elaborate facades to hide their painful feelings of loneliness.

Abandoned by People

Sarah described her relationship with her cold, rigid, demanding husband. She longed for intimacy and affection, but what she got was a perfunctory physical relationship, enough money for groceries, and shallow conversation. In return, he expected her to keep the house spotless, cook like a French chef, and drop whatever she was doing to do whatever he wanted her to. Her conclusion, like most codependents, was that the problem was her fault. "I guess I'm just not a good person," she said weakly, looking down. "I guess I'm not worthy of being loved." She began to cry.

Abusive or addicted people usually give a little and take a lot. In contrast, the codependent is like a tank of water with a slow drip coming in and a stream going out. For a while, the tank will flow, but eventually it will run dry. The trickle can never fill the tank as long as there is a hole in the bottom. The codependent may get a little encouragement, but he gives so much more time and emotional energy that he is effectually "running on empty."

As the codependent gives and gives, a destructive sense of *entitlement* grows within him. He feels entitled to the appreciation and respect of others. Getting strokes becomes a compulsion. When he gets that appreciation and respect, he is satisfied like an alcoholic taking a drink. When he doesn't get it, he feels angry and abandoned.

We feel condemned. We feel controlled. We feel confused. We feel lonely. We feel angry, but we can't say anything or we might experience even more condemnation, manipulation, and loneliness. We feel hopelessly trapped.

Afraid of our emotions, we stuff them and act like nothing is wrong. We are unwilling to say how we feel—that we are hurt and angry—because we are afraid that people will withdraw from us. We're afraid they will go away, and we'll be even more lonely. Even worse, if we don't act like we appreciate what they say and do, they will probably get angry with us, and that risk is simply too great. We are lonely now. We don't want to feel any more so.

Although we are desperate for intimacy, we don't feel lovable, and we're afraid of losing what little warmth we already have. The combination of these factors paralyzes and confuses us. One young lady who described her loneliness, desires, and fears seemed like a little girl who was crying, "I need help! Leave me alone!"

Many of us are so crushed and have such a low sense of value that we can't even accept genuine love and affirmation. I encouraged a woman with a very painful family background—Rhonda—to find a friend who could share her hurts and joys. I knew of a mutual friend, Sandy, who really loved her and who wanted to pursue a relationship with her. It looked like a perfect situation! Month after month passed, but Rhonda only developed a superficial relationship with Sandy. My encouragement didn't seem to help the situation.

After a long time, I decided to ask the hard questions again. "Rhonda, Sandy really loves you. She wants to be the kind of friend to you that we've talked about. Why don't you open up to her and let her be your friend?"

Rhonda looked very sad. "I can't. I just can't. I'm afraid that if she really knew me, she wouldn't like me."

In the same way, codependents have difficulty accepting compliments. They don't believe they are worthy of praise (even though they desperately want to be affirmed), so they explain away their successes, shift the compliment to someone else (someone "more deserving"), or in some other way discount what they have done. They long for appreciation, but when it comes they feel they are unworthy of it. They remain lonely, feeling abandoned and empty.

Abandoned by God

The unconditional love, forgiveness, and acceptance of God is the message codependents need, but instead, most feel distant from Him. They feel that He, too, doesn't approve of them, and that they can't do enough to please Him no matter how hard they try.

This compounds the codependent's feelings of hopelessness, pain, and loneliness because God is seen as his last hope: *If He doesn't love me, who will?* The codependent's view of God is almost always the same as his view of his parents. If his parents neglected him, he will feel that God doesn't care. If his parents condemned him, he will feel that God is harsh and demanding. However his parents treated him is the perception he has of God, who then is seen as part of the problem, not the solution.

Codependent Christians tend (as usual) to be one of two extremes. Their desire for intimacy with God is either squelched by a view that God is cool, distant, and harsh, or they sense the love of God to an extreme depth and become "hypermystical" and feelings-oriented. As in every other area of their lives, they lack objectivity and balance, and react as extremists.

Jeff's mother was harsh and demanding. His father escaped by working long hours, developing friends outside the neighborhood, and being passive at home. When Jeff became a Christian in his early twenties, he felt the love and acceptance he had always wanted. This feeling came from both his relationship with the Lord and his relationship with other Christians. It seemed to be heaven on earth!

But after a few months, Jeff's warm feelings about God began to fade. The way he had learned to cope at home was to do everything his mother wanted him to, but of course nothing could please her. Now he began to feel that he wasn't quite as accepted and loved by the Lord, so he unconsciously began to act toward God the same way that he had acted toward his mother. He tried to do whatever he could to please Him. That solution led him only to empty perfectionism before; now it led him to strict legalism. There seemed to be plenty of people at church who knew lots of things Jeff ought to do to please God, so he tried to do them all. He attended every meeting, read the Bible religiously, and gave away lots of money, but instead of feeling closer to God, he felt that God was increasingly distant, harsh, and demanding. His *want-to* freshness in those first months of his relationship with the Lord had become a stifling, condemning, *have-to* burden. Though he did a lot *for* God, he seemed to feel more and more distant *from* God.

Abandoned by Authority

Codependents tend to view authority the same way they view the addicted or abusive people in their lives, especially if those people are parents. They are often intensely loyal to their parents, bosses, pastors or other kinds of leaders, and in their black-or-white perception (or lack thereof), they sometimes believe that the one in authority can do no wrong. They make others omnipotent because they feel so inadequate themselves. They will put up with all kinds of mistakes until, at last, the pendulum swings and the authority figure who could do no wrong suddenly can do nothing right.

Beneath this is the paradox that the codependent wants to be accepted and appreciated by those who are in positions of importance and respect, so he values their opinions of him highly; in fact, too highly. But he also has an innate sense that those in authority are out to get him, to use him, and to manipulate him. Depending on which end of these extremes the pendulum has swung, he sees that authority as either black or white, either for or against him.

On the black side, he feels misunderstood, abused, and abandoned. Even the slightest disagreement is interpreted as, *They just don't understand me! They don't care about me at all!*

Steve was a loyal lieutenant as an agent at a real estate company. He worked hard and sold a lot of homes. He usually had good insights at sales meetings and his opinion was respected. But after three years, the brokers made a series of decisions that he disagreed with. For a while, there was no problem, but a rift developed as Steve interpreted these disagreements as personal attacks against him. The casual friendship he had enjoyed with the brokers evaporated rather quickly as Steve withdrew from them. He became more intense, and he began making subtle jabs about his bosses to the other agents. If they agreed with his comments, he would take them aside and explain how wrong the brokers were and how obviously right he was. He could hardly sleep at night, thinking about each person in the office, from the secretaries to the agents, who had been with the company for a long time. How could he get them to see how reasonable he was, and how could he get them to take his side?

A few weeks of Steve's lobbying and smear campaign resulted in an insurrection at the office. A sales meeting turned into an "us against them" fight as Steve and the people he had won to his side argued vehemently against the people who had once been their friends and coworkers, but now were their enemies. There was no turning back. Steve demanded that the company take his advice. They didn't. Instead, they fired him.

Whether Steve had been right or wrong about the issues was not the question. Steve had interpreted disagreement as a personal attack. He tried to defend himself by gathering together people who would agree with him, and then led them in a black-and-white approach that only caused alienation, not reason and reconciliation. Disagreement made him feel misunderstood, used, and abandoned by those in authority.

Facades

People often develop facades in childhood as a survival technique. Looking calm, cheerful, or tough enabled them to shield their feelings. Although these facades protected them in the past, they are detrimental in the long run because they prevent the development of honest and genuine relationships.

Codependents desperately want to be understood and to feel close to others, but they're afraid. They're afraid to take the risks of involving themselves in relationships because they might be rejected. Then they would hurt even more. To avoid this risk, to avoid more pain, they protect themselves by appearing to be happy and well adjusted even when they are dying inside. They erect facades.

Hiding behind these facades, we don't say what we mean, and we don't mean what we say. To put it bluntly, we lie a lot. We say yes, when we want to say no. We say we are just fine, when we are feeling just a step or two away from suicide.

We say we want to go somewhere because we think going there will make someone else happy enough to like us, when in fact, we don't want to go there at all. We get so wrapped up in other people's desires and making other people happy that we get numb and confused, and don't even know what we want! We are so busy making other people feel good that we don't even know what we feel!

We exaggerate. We make good things a little bit better so people will be a little more impressed with us, and we make bad things a little worse so people will feel sorry for us. It usually works, but it's lying.

We offer to help with a friendly smile even when we're so angry with that person we could spit nails. If our countenance slips and someone asks, "Is anything wrong?" we give an excuse that is usually partially true, but which keeps others at arms-length: "Oh, I have a headache today," or "Yeah, I'm just not having a good day, but I'm all right."

We become masterful at selling ourselves. We are enthusiastic about our jobs, our families, how well we're doing, our new hairstyles and clothes. We find something that's good and milk it for all it's worth so that people will believe we are really doing well. But in reflective moments, we realize that what we've said is a lie, that our facade is a lie—but we can't let them know the truth! As a result, we often feel dirty, guilty, and alone.

Our motto becomes: *The truth hurts, so avoid it. If people knew me, they'd reject me.* So we develop elaborate and usually unconscious facades to avoid the truth and to keep people from knowing how much we hurt and how angry we really are. These facades may protect us from the risks of intimacy, but they leave us lonely. When we lock others out, we lock ourselves in.

Questions

1. Why does a person who devotes himself to rescuing and serving often feel lonely?

2. How does a lonely person think and feel about himself?

3. How does he think and feel about others?

4. What are some reasons why many of us feel that taking the risk of self-disclosure and intimacy is too great?

5. In what ways do you feel:

   a) Abandoned by people?

   b) Abandoned by God?

c) Abandoned by authority?

6. What facades do you use to keep people away? What are the results of using these?

Nine

The Codependent Christian

The Gospel of Jesus Christ is a message of freedom, forgiveness, hope, love, joy, and strength. It is the Good News, the most liberating and energizing power mankind has ever, or will ever hear! Through the distorted glasses of codependency, however, this phenomenal message is often seen as oppressive, condemning, and guilt-inducing. Freedom is turned to bondage, forgiveness to guilt, hope to despair, love to condemnation, joy to pessimism, and divine strength to self-sufficiency.

But why? Why is it so difficult for the codependent Christian to understand and apply God's grace?

Ought's and Should's

As we have seen, codependents have a warped sense of responsibility. Since they perceive that their worth comes from their ability to perform, they are driven either to achieve as much as possible or to withdraw in hopelessness. But how does a person measure his performance so he can see if he has achieved value and worth? By doing what he *should* do. By doing what he *ought* to do, and by dividing life into distinct categories: the "have-to's" and the "can't's." This black-and-white definition steals the fun and spontaneity from life and leaves a person with an overactive conscience; pride if he has done well, despair if he hasn't, and a fear of failure and rejection no matter how well he has done. The codependent who is a Christian carries not only society's ought's and should's, he also adds the ought's and should's of Christianity to his already oppressive load. Instead of helping him to overcome his oppression, his wrong perspective of Christ and the Christian life oppresses him even further. Instead of grace, he experiences guilt. It is grace that ultimately produces a "want-to" motivation, though it may take a long time to develop.

A pastor who is a friend of mine lamented that he could teach for twenty-nine minutes on the love and grace of God, finishing with only one minute of application of obedience in light of that grace, and some people in the congregation would leave having heard only the last minute. The majority would completely miss the bulk of the message and the careful context of grace that couched the call to obedience. Instead, what they heard was guilt and condemnation. This pastor was deeply saddened that these people had missed the motivation for obedience.

Another teacher presented a Sunday school class series on *The Search for Significance*, a book and workbook which contains over 400 pages explaining the love, forgiveness, acceptance, and grace of God. Most of those in the class were encouraged and motivated by his talks and discussions, but he was chagrined that several people had just the opposite response. They somehow couldn't hear the liberating message of the material. They only heard that they had to do more and do better to be accepted by God—the exact antithesis of the material!

The codependent Christian divorces grace—the source of perspective and power—from the high moral and ethical expectations of the Bible. He then feels obliged to meet these higher expectations, but has only guilt motivation and his own will to achieve them. And the more he reads the Bible, the clearer these expectations and others become, increasing his sense of guilt.

There are many commands in the Scriptures that the codependent Christian misinterprets and applies in his savior mode to gain a sense of worth. Some of these include:

- going the second mile to help someone
- turning the other cheek when someone hurts him
- loving those who don't love him
- giving cheerfully
- denying his own desires for the sake of others
- loving his neighbor as he loves himself
- having a disciplined life of prayer and Bible study
- letting no unwholesome word proceed from his mouth
- forgiving, loving, and accepting others as Christ does
- generally speaking, the worse a person treats him, the more he joyfully serves him or her

The codependent Christian believes that he is expected to perform these commands (and all the others) perfectly, with feelings of love, peace, and joy at all times. In the Christian life, he surmises, there is absolutely no room for hurt and anger.

His plight is further complicated by this denial of emotions. His hurt and anger are stuffed away with reasoning like: *A good Christian shouldn't feel this way...so I won't. It's so wonderful to be a Christian... (but I'm dying inside).*

Sooner or later, despair will catch up with him, and his thoughts will become something like this:

If I were walking with God, I wouldn't have these problems.
God has deserted me.
Nobody cares about me. I'm all alone.
Maybe I'm not really a Christian after all. Surely nobody who feels this way can be a Christian.

But at the same time, he will often defend God so that no one will think badly of Him. Just as the codependent denies his hurt and anger, and excuses and defends the person in his life who has hurt him, he also tries to deny the hurt and anger he perceives that God has caused. And he tries to make sure that God doesn't get any blame for his calamity. In the codependent's eyes, the Savior needs a savior.

The Scriptures and Codependency

Codependents have a strange view of the Scriptures. Their distorted "have-to" perspective makes them believe that care-taking and enabling are virtues. They are not.

Russ's friend, Ben, called to ask for a favor. "Russ, I'm in a real jam. I need some money. I've had some unexpected expenses lately that just blindsided me. I haven't known what in the world to do, man, but I knew I could count on you."

Russ snapped into his savior mode with that last statement.

"Can you let me have $700 until next week? I *promise* I'll pay you back next Friday. What do you say, Russ, this would really help me out, and I don't have anybody else to count on."

Russ quickly thought through a few passages of Scripture: *give cheerfully* (2 Cor. 9:7), *give without asking anything in return* (Luke 6:30-35), and *give liberally* (Rom. 12:8).

"Of course, Ben." Russ had concluded what the Lord wanted him to do. "I'll have to go by and get this out of our savings. Would you like me to bring a check by tonight?"

But the next Friday, Ben didn't call. Russ was disappointed, but he remembered that Luke 6:30 says not to ask for the money back. A few days later, the phone rang again. It was Ben.

"Russ, old buddy, how's it going? Man, I'm really in bad shape. Listen, I'll tell you something if you promise not to tell my wife. Okay?"

"Okay, I guess so. What is it, Ben?"

"Somebody in the church just beat me out of $500. That's part of the money I was going to use to pay you back, but now I'm in real trouble. I know I shouldn't ask you for it, but Russ, I'm desperate and I know you're the only person I can turn to. Can you let me borrow another $500? Man, I'll get it back to you next week *for sure.*"

Russ remembered the scripture passage. Then he thought, *That $500 would really put my wife and me in a shaky situation if anything* *should happen, but what can I do now? I have to do what the Scriptures say.*

"Sure Ben, when do you need it?"

But after weeks, months, and now years, Russ hasn't seen the money. It really did put him and his family in a financial bind, but hadn't he followed the teaching of the Scriptures? Hadn't he done what was right?

In his desire to help, Russ fell into the trap of enabling. You see, Ben was addicted to prescription drugs and he needed the money to keep up his habit. Russ didn't think to ask a couple of hard questions, questions that would expose reality. He would have helped Ben a lot more if he had asked those questions, checked with his wife (why had he been so secretive about her?), and then asked himself the question, *What will really help Ben?* This lack of objectivity, coupled with a habit of enabling as a savior, had led Russ to misinterpret and misapply the Scriptures.

If codependency so distorts the Christian faith that freedom becomes slavery, should the codependent throw out the Scriptures? Is codependency an excuse to disobey the Lord? No!

The Word of God, the Spirit of God, and the people of God are the tools He has given us to effectively change our behavior, but it takes perception and understanding to overcome our blindness and emerge from the eclipse of codependency. The truth of the Word of God, energized by the Spirit of God, in the loving and affirming context of the people of God, enables the codependent Christian to be freed from his bondage.

When I first began to study codependency, I wondered, *If codependency is such a problem, why don't the Scriptures say anything about it?* Then I realized, they do! Changing warped, codependent perceptions relates directly to the dominant themes of the Bible: the character of God, the grace of God, His unconditional love and acceptance—which is not based on our performance—His declaration of our worth and value because of our identity in Christ, helping people for right reasons, etc. These transforming truths are not communicated in the language of 20th century psychology, but in that of the ancient writers. Still, they speak powerfully to the root needs of codependents: the needs for love, acceptance, worth, and value.

The writers of the Scriptures went to great lengths to teach about the character of God, our identity, how we relate to others, and our motivations for obedience. In *The Search for Significance,* Robert McGee outlines several of these motivations in the Scriptures, which include:[1]

- The love of Christ motivates us to obey.
- Sin is destructive.
- The Father will discipline us in love.
- His commands for us are good.
- We will receive rewards.
- Obedience is our opportunity to honor God.

As you can see, guilt is not one of these motivations! Neither is the desire to be accepted! Nor the fear of punishment! There are many good motives found in the Bible, but they are centered on a right view of God and a proper view of our identity as His beloved children. This results in "want-to," not "have-to" motivations.

If you are a codependent, you may have concluded that the commands of Scripture are wrong and harmful. As you begin (or continue) the process of changing your view of God and of the Scriptures, you will see that God is not like the harsh, manipulative, or neglectful person in your life. Nor are you a terrible, worthless person who always has to be more, do more, and say more to be accepted. Yes, you are a sinner, but you are a sinner who has been redeemed by Christ, adopted as a dearly beloved child of God, and given the incredible privilege of knowing, loving, and serving Him.

The traits of the codependent Christian are remarkably similar to those of a codependent who is not a believer. One group of Christians who are trying to help each other with the pangs of codependency is a group called Sinners Anonymous. Here is that organization's chart of a codependent Christian's characteristics:

Symptoms	Growing Discoveries
1. Living in confused unreality	1. A growing sense of being not real and inadequate
2. Lonely and isolated	2. Bonded; connected, a sense of "family" in program
3. Being grandiose or depressed	3. Moderation and balance
4. Being lost; no sense of purpose for life; intense but not productive	4. A sense of purpose and direction
5. Baffling "denial" which is seen by other people but not myself	5. Awareness of control behaviors
6. Hopeless fear of being overwhelmed	6. Being afraid much of the time, but inside feeling hope and serenity
7. Fear of other people and of expressing my opinions and reality to them	7. The courage to stand for what I believe and to state simply what I am feeling
8. Self-centered and manipulative control devices which happen automatically and lead to broken and bruised relationships	8. God-centered, concrete acts expressing care for other people
9. Need to control people, places, and things to get what I want when I want it, and to keep fear level down	9. Being able to let go, trust God with the outcome, and feel security even with problems unsolved
10. A sense of being lost and of covering up since I don't know who I am	10. A sense of identity in being God's child. A sense of discovery in who I really am
11. Dishonesty and devious ways of getting things done	11. Honest and direct, often making quick amends when I am dishonest

12. Trying to get close to God by an organized religiousness	12. A spiritual recovery and discovery that humility has to do with transparency and integrity
13. Self-righteousness in believing I know what's best for people	13. Humility and an awareness that I'm responsible only for my own feelings and my own recovery—not that I am the boss of the family and of others
14. Promoting and talking publicly about what I believe	14. Living the experience of recovery in my own life when I'm alone and not "on stage"
15. Being overcommitted and always taking on more things than I can handle	15. The freedom to have boundaries and say no when I have "enough on my plate"
16. Chaos	16. Serenity and peace
17. Despair	17. Joy

Superficial Solutions

Lacking objectivity and being performance-oriented, we look for quick, simple solutions to fix ourselves and other people. There's only one problem—they don't work! Oh, they may work for a few people for a while, but codependency does not lend itself to quick, simple solutions precisely because it is a deep, long-term problem, and not primarily one of wrong action. That could be corrected relatively easily. Ours is a problem of perception.

Instead of helping codependents with their warped perspectives, both society and the Christian culture usually *reinforce* codependency by valuing codependent behavior. Helping, fixing, enabling, being intense, easily motivated (manipulated), effective, conscientious, and pleasing others are considered virtues! Codependents often make the best employees and church workers because they are effective, loyal, and intense. In some Christian circles, the obsessive-compulsive drive of codependency is equated with a deep commitment to Christ! These two may seem similar on the outside. The activities, words, and habits may be similar, but on the inside they are leagues apart. One is dominated by guilt, introspection, and the need to achieve to gain worth. The other is a response to the unconditional love and acceptance of God.

We hear and read that the answer is to "deny yourself," but in the context of a broken identity in codependency, denying yourself just becomes another way of enabling, fixing, and not having an identity. The Christian who is told to deny himself should also be told that he is greatly valued, deeply loved, and accepted. In that context, denying himself is not work, but true worship.

One woman I know is seen by most people as the archetype of Christian maturity. But one day she confided to me that she feels driven to say, be, and do the right things to win the approval from others that she never received from her father. She is an outstanding Bible student, she is a gifted organizer, and an activist in evangelism and discipleship. She is always ready to help others, and she does an excellent job of it, too! But there is a nagging, gnawing emptiness in her heart that all of these activities can't fill.

Why do we remain this way? Why do we go from one quick, easy solution to the next, wondering why they work for other people (do they?) but not for us? One reason is that we lack perception, so we don't see a choice. Seen through the distorted glasses of codependency, our thoughts, feelings, and behavior appear to be the only game in town. Another reason is our fear of the unknown. We cling to our painful, empty solutions in fear that something else may be even more painful and more empty.

In this fear and denial, we believe others' promises and lies because we can't see the truth and are afraid the truth will hurt too much. We gloss over the offenses of others (even though they may have hurt us deeply) and we "forgive and forget." But this seemingly godly response actually is codependent behavior because it is designed to cover up our pain and excuse the offender. True forgiveness recognizes the truth in all of its pain and ugliness, seeks to help the person see the underlying problem that caused the offense, and then perseveres in the relationship. That is a far cry from the denial and quick-fix tendency of codependent forgiveness.

Superficial solutions sound so good. They seem to help so many people. But in the long run, quick, easy answers only prolong and exacerbate the problems of codependency. Real answers are needed that speak to the real issues of worth and identity. These solutions should be experienced in a long process so they will sink in deeply and profoundly. In the next section of the book, we will explore our identity in Christ and the profound impact of healthy relationships in the healing process. We will also learn how to identify codependent behavior, how to detach to gain objectivity, and how to make good, healthy decisions.

Questions

1. What things do you feel that you *have* to do as a Christian to feel better about yourself?

2. What are some ways that the Scriptures can be misapplied to feed codependent behavior?

3. How does codependency affect:

   a) Your view of God?

   b) Your identity and worth?

   c) Your relationships with others?

   d) The standards and rules you set for yourself?

4. What are your dominant motivations for obedience?

5. What are some superficial solutions you can think of (such as: "Just pray about it," or "Spend one hour with the Lord everyday.") for codependency?

6. Why don't these superficial solutions work?

PART TWO

THE SOLUTION

Ten

Identity: A Sense of Worth

Robert walked in at a friend's party, and after exchanging the usual pleasantries with several people, he was approached by Melanie. "Robert, what's new with you these days?"

Robert had been learning a lot about his codependency and how it had affected him. He had also made some major strides in developing a new identity. He replied with a smile, "Do you really want to know—it will take a while to explain—or would you rather have me say, 'Not much'?"

"Okay, I'll bite." Melanie was curious now. "What *is* going on with you?"

Robert leaned against a wall and began, "It's kind of hard to give all the details, but maybe a *Cliff Notes* version will do. Over the past few months I've been realizing how my family has affected me. My mother is an alcoholic, and I've always felt responsible for making her happy, but no matter what I did, it never seemed good enough to please her. Now I'm becoming a new person!"

"What do you mean?" Melanie was confused. "You look the same to me."

"I've been trying to help others so much all my life that I've been like a puppet on a string. A couple of months ago, I realized that I've always tried to be the person that other people have wanted me to be. I've never really been myself. In fact, I haven't been myself for forty-three years—until lately! I've been *me* for about a month now, and I like it!"

Robert's insights and new sense of identity are common to people who are emerging from the eclipse of codependency. This emergence is not instantaneous, however. It is a process. This section of the book is entitled "The Solution," but the solution is not just a formula that we can immediately apply and all will be well. The solution has certain ingredients which must be seen in the context of a long and often difficult process.

The changes that need to occur in a codependent's life (changes in his perception of God, his perception of himself, his perception of others, and his lifestyle), require a blend of four components: cognitive, relational, mystical, and temporal, or time. We need to know the truth about ourselves, God, and others; the cognitive aspect. This truth needs to be modeled to us by others, and we need them to encourage, affirm, and correct us; the relational part. But even this is not enough. We need the Lord to work in our lives to give us wisdom, to give us courage to take steps of faith, and to give us power to fight the uphill battle of codependency. And finally, we need time. We live in a society marked by speed, with automated tellers and drive-through banking, fast food, fast sex, telecommunications, microwaves, and more. But years of believing certain things about yourself, God, and others are not changed in an instant! It takes time. Most of us, however, are very impatient. We want change. We want it to be complete. And we want it NOW!

It is counterproductive to expect too much too soon. That usually leads to discouragement and even abandoning the process. Hang in there. The process may be long, and it will be full of ups and downs, but there is hope for change. Now, after that warning, let's examine our identity and sense of worth.

The Codependent's Identity

I asked Sharon a couple of questions: "How would you describe yourself? What adjectives would you use?"

Sharon thought for a minute, then she said slowly, "That's hard for me. I guess I'd say: 'warm, outgoing'...things like that."

"What else?"

After a long pause, she said, "Stupid, ugly...I hate the way I look! I hate the way I act! I hate everything about me!" Sharon put her head in her hands and cried. Her identity, her self-concept, and her sense of worth were clouded and darkened by her codependency.

As we have seen, codependents have been deprived of a sense of value. The unconditional love and acceptance we need has been withdrawn from us to some extent, and we attempt to get our worth by rescuing, helping, pleasing, and being successful. But no matter how well we perform, these solutions only give short-term satisfaction. They ultimately lead to more pain and emptiness because our best seldom seems to be good enough.

The three primary and three corollary characteristics of codependency give us a window to see how codependency affects our sense of worth. Let's take a brief look at these again in this context:

Primary Characteristics of Codependency

Lack of Objectivity: We are so busy rescuing or withdrawing that we don't see the truth about our lives and circumstances. The truth seems to be too painful to cope with, so we continue to try the same old, ineffective, and painful solution: pleasing others so they will love us.

A Warped Sense of Responsibility: We play the roles of savior and/or Judas, rescuing to earn a sense of value or withdrawing to avoid the pain of rejection and failure.

Controlled/Controlling: We act like puppets, doing whatever others want us to, trying desperately to please them. In turn, we try to control our own lives so we can avoid failure, and we try to control others so that they will contribute to our success and our ability to win approval.

Corollary Characteristics of Codependency

Hurt and Anger: We feel hurt when we are condemned, manipulated, or neglected, and become angry with the one who hurt us. We repress these painful emotions, only to have them emerge in displaced anger, disproportionate anger, or depression.

Guilt: If we attempt to get our worth from being good and pleasing people, then any failure—or even perceived failure—leads to intense pangs of guilt. We are ashamed of ourselves. We are driven to do better, to do more, and to analyze our every thought, emotion, action, and relationship to see if we can improve.

Loneliness: We desperately want to be loved, so we try to make people happy, make them successful, and make them feel good. Then, we surmise, they will love us. But even when others seem to like us, we still live in fear that we might do something they might not like.

Even this cursory glance at the identity of a codependent reveals that his sense of value is based entirely on his ability to perform and please others. That perspective is deep and strong, but it is a dead end. It leads only to more pain, more obsessive-compulsive behavior, and more emptiness. It is a false hope, but the Scriptures give us another solution.

Biblical Identity

If someone asked, "Who are you?" how would you answer? We usually think of our identity in terms of our function in society. We say, "I'm a salesman." "I'm a mother of three boys." "I'm a lawyer." *...a student ...a secretary.* Or maybe we would say, "I'm an American"...*a Republican ...a Democrat ...a Christian.*

When the apostle John wanted to identity himself in his gospel, he did so relationally. He referred to himself as *the disciple whom Jesus loved* (John 13:23; 21:7, 20). John's sense of being loved and accepted by Christ was so strong that this was how he identified himself.

When the apostle Paul wrote to the churches, he put a great deal of emphasis on teaching the believers about their identity. As a general rule, the first half of each letter is about identity; the second half, specific applications of that identity. His circular letter to the believers in Ephesus is particularly instructive. The first three chapters clearly explain our identity in Christ. Let's take a look at part of the first chapter:

Paul, an apostle of Christ Jesus by the will of God, to the saints who are at Ephesus, and who are faithful in Christ Jesus: Grace to you and peace from God our Father and the Lord Jesus Christ. Blessed be the God and Father of our Lord Jesus Christ, who has blessed us with every spiritual blessing in the heavenly places in Christ, just as He chose us in Him before the foundation of the world, that we should be holy and blameless before Him. In love He predestined us to adoption as sons through Jesus Christ to Himself, according to the kind intention of His will, to the praise of the glory of His grace, which He freely bestowed on us in the Beloved. In Him we have redemption through His blood, the forgiveness of our trespasses, according to the riches of His grace, which He lavished upon us... In Him, you also, after listening to the message of truth, the gospel of your salvation—having also believed, you were sealed in Him with the Holy Spirit of promise, who is given as a pledge of our inheritance, with a view to the redemption of God's own possession, to the praise of His glory. Eph. 1:1-8,13-14

Several key words in this passage relate to our identity:

Chosen

Verse four states that as believers, we have been *chosen* by God. But why? Were we chosen because we are smart, good-looking, rich, efficient, or some other trait? No, we have been chosen so that we can be declared *holy and blameless before Him:* not perfect in our behavior, but secure in our identity. One of the ways I like to communicate this sense of being chosen to my children is to say to them: "If somebody lined up all the little girls and little boys in the whole world and told me that I could pick one of each, do you know who I'd choose?"

Catherine and Taylor usually smile and say, "Who, Daddy?"

I wave my finger around the room like I'm surveying the millions of children in the world, then I quickly point to them and say, "You, that's who I'd choose. Do you know why?"

They grin and ask, "No, Daddy, why?"

"Just because I love you." They really enjoy my doing this, and I think it communicates to them how very much I value them.

Adopted

Verse five states that we, as Christians, have been adopted by God. We usually use the term *child of God* without thinking about it, but He didn't have to adopt us. He could have left us as helpless and hopeless people. He could have made us His slaves. He could have obliterated us in His righteous wrath. But He didn't. He adopted us like the Romans adopted a person, as an adult child with full privileges as an heir. A good picture of this is in the movie *Ben Hur.* As a slave, Judah Ben Hur was adopted by the Roman admiral, Arias. Judah Ben Hur was granted full sonship, given a ring to signify his place in the family, and accepted and loved by Arias.

Forgiven

As Christians, we have been forgiven (verse seven). Christ's death is the complete payment for our sins. Those wrongs that condemn us as guilty before God have been paid in full. We are not just excused and our sins waved off by a benevolent grandfather figure. These sins demand payment, the awful payment of Christ's death on the cross. How much are we forgiven? The verse says *according to the riches of His grace.*

There is no sin too great, no offense too bad (except refusing to accept Christ's payment for sin) that it is unforgivable.

Sealed

The seal of Rome (verse thirteen) signified ownership and security. When Christ was put in the tomb, the Pharisees asked Pilate to make it secure so no one could steal the body and say that Jesus was raised from the dead. Matthew's gospel records Pilate's directive:

> *Pilate said to them, "You have a guard; go, make it as secure as you know how." And they went and made the grave secure, and along with the guard they set a seal on the stone.*
> Matt. 27:65-66

That seal was the ultimate in Roman security, yet it could not keep Christ from His resurrection.

Paul used the idea of a seal to express the believer's security in Christ. The Holy Spirit's seal is the ultimate in spiritual security, but unlike the Roman seal, it cannot be broken. This seal signifies that we have been bought by the blood of Christ (1Cor. 6:19-20), so we are owned by God. Also, it means that we are secure in our relationship with Him. If we have trusted in Christ as our Savior and have experienced His forgiveness and adoption, then He will never drop us, lose us, or reject us.

Paul wrote to the believers in Rome:

> *For I am convinced that neither death, nor life, nor angels, nor principalities, nor things present, nor things to come, nor powers, nor height, nor depth, nor any other created thing, shall be able to separate us from the love of God, which is in Christ Jesus our Lord.*
> Rom. 8:38-39

We are secure because we have been sealed by the Holy Spirit.

There are many other passages about our identity in Christ, but we will not go into them all. Perhaps this chart will give a little more insight into the truth of our identity in Christ. On the left is a list of some characteristics of people who haven't trusted Christ. On the right are some traits of those who have trusted in Christ. The transition is succinctly stated in Col. 1:13-14:

> *For He delivered us from the domain of darkness, and transferred us to the kingdom of His beloved Son, in whom we have redemption, the forgiveness of sins.*

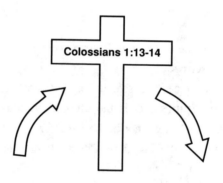

Identity apart from Christ	Identity as children of God
helpless, ungodly sinners, deserving wrath, enemies of God (Rom. 5:6-10)	*justified* - completely forgiven (Rom. 3:21-26)
hostile, evil deeds, alienated (Col. 1:21)	*reconciled* - totally accepted (Col. 1:19-22)
self-righteous (Rom. 1-2, Titus 3:7-11)	*propitiated* - deeply loved (1 John 4:9-11)
without hope (Eph. 2:12)	*redeemed* - bought by Christ's blood (1 Cor. 6:19-20)
destined for eternal condemnation (2 Thess. 1:6-10)	*no condemnation* (Rom. 8:1)
	near to God (1 Pet. 2:10)
	choice and precious (1 Pet. 2:4-5)
	soldier for Christ (2 Tim. 2:3-4)
	ambassador for Christ (2 Cor. 5:20)

The Character of God

Codependents seem to have a consistently inaccurate view of God. In our book, *The Parent Factor*, Robert McGee, Jim Craddock, and I explain that a person's view of God is shaped by his relationship with his parents. In codependent, dysfunctional families, the children grow up with a distorted view of God. If their parents were (or are) abusive, they will probably believe that God is harsh and condemning. If their parents are neglectful, they will probably believe that God doesn't care about them. Similarly, spouses of compulsive persons can have their view of God adversely affected by that relationship.[1]

The clear teaching of Scripture is that God is not like anybody or anything! He is far more loving, far more powerful, far more kind, strong, and interested in us than we can imagine.

One of the painful ironies of codependency is that the only consistent, loving One whom we can always count on for unconditional love, acceptance, wisdom, and strength is seen through our distorted lenses as harsh, mean, demanding, and distant. We need to have our view of God changed, but again, it took years to develop that misperception. It will take time to develop a correct one.

As you read these pages about the love, forgiveness, and acceptance of God, which He has demonstrated by the death of Christ to pay for our sins, you may realize that you have only gone through the motions, and have never begun a relationship with Him. Take some time to reflect on the passages of Scripture listed in this chapter. Then, if you want to, express your desire to the Lord to have your sins forgiven and to begin a relationship with Him. You can use your own words, or you can pray something like this:

> *Lord Jesus, I need You. Thank You for dying on the cross to pay for my sins. I want to receive You as my Savior and Lord. Thank You for forgiving me and giving me eternal life.*

133

I want to know You better and experience Your love and grace. Make me the kind of person You want me to be.

The moment that you place your faith in Christ, all of the truths that we have examined in this chapter will be true of you! You will be adopted, forgiven, sealed, and secure! Reflect on His work, and trust Him to change your view of yourself, Him, and others.

Applying the Truth of God's Word

Fighting the old battles of codependency in the same old way while wearing distorted glasses yields the same old results: dashed hopes, more pain, and more emptiness. Just trying harder to be successful and to please people isn't the answer. We need a new battle plan.

After Pearl Harbor, the Japanese controlled a huge area of the South Pacific. They held many heavily fortified islands in their push toward Australia. General Douglas McArthur, commander of the Allied forces in the Pacific, decided on a bold and daring new plan. He didn't attack where most military experts advised him to attack. He bypassed the fortified islands and attacked islands behind the Japanese perimeter. His forces established strong points of their own, and forced the Japanese to retreat.

We should do the same. Our strategy should not be to try harder, make more people happy, get more done, be more in control, or rescue more. We need a bold new plan to expose and attack the root of our need: our identity and sense of worth.

For many of us, the truth of who we are in Christ is not new. We have known it for years. We can quote passage after passage, but the Scriptures haven't penetrated past our denial-ridden, codependent Christian facade. We need a fresh look, perhaps through honest people who are struggling with real issues, and who are more interested in real solutions than easy answers. We may not need to change our beliefs about our identity, but we may need to change the depth to which we apply these truths.

Some passages of Scripture play havoc on the codependent. Interpreted through his distorted vision, they produce more guilt and pain instead of freedom and joyful obedience. One example of this is a passage where Jesus instructs His disciples to "deny" themselves:

> *Then Jesus said to His disciples, "If anyone wishes to come after Me, let him deny himself, and take up his cross, and follow Me."*
>
> Matt. 16:24

In the context of this verse, we see that Jesus has just rebuked Peter.

> *But He turned and said to Peter, "Get behind Me, Satan! You are a stumbling block to Me; for you are not setting your mind on God's interests, but man's."*
>
> Matt. 16:23

So Jesus' instruction to deny ourselves is in the context of giving up our selfish desires. This is confusing for the codependent because he has denied himself and given up his own desires all of his life, and here Jesus seems to be telling him to do it some more! But the reason he has denied himself and given up his desires is to gain approval and identity, not to offer true service to the Lord. The codependent needs a new identity, a strong sense of being loved and accepted by God and by His people. Then denying his own desires will make sense. Until then, he will only be feeding his own codependent habits of rescuing and serving to gain approval.

I am not suggesting that this passage (and others like it) do not apply to codependents, but that the codependent's distortions about God and himself (like the Pharisees' distortions about God and about themselves) need to be corrected. He needs a new identity based on the clear teaching and application of the Scriptures. Then, instead of feeding his codependency, his service and obedience will truly honor Christ.

We need to be reminded (often!) of our new identity. A friend of mine writes little notes to his codependent wife to encourage her: "You are a person who has great value and tremendous worth—just by being you!" Communication like that almost always strikes a chord in our minds and hearts, but sadly it is rare.

The application of these truths in a relationship of love and affirmation is like light and salt to codependents. In this context, we learn to face the truth about ourselves, God, and others. We learn that we have only limited responsibility in the lives of others. It isn't up to us to make people happy. We learn to have our own desires and dreams, and we learn to let other people make their own decisions. We learn to be honest about our emotions: our pain of rejection, intense anger, and disappointments as well as our love and hope. We learn that it's okay to fail because our sense of worth is not threatened by failure, and we learn to try for the right reasons. And finally, we learn to love and be loved, to be honest with people, and to give and receive in relationships.

But remember, this doesn't happen all at once. It's like peeling an onion. Each layer brings new revelations, new fears, new hopes, and new changes in our lives. Often, we find ourselves dealing repeatedly with the same issues, but it is often at a deeper level or layer. You may be discouraged that there are *so many layers!* But take heart. Be glad you are in the process of healing. That process, with all of its joys and pains, is a sign of progress. The flashes of insight and surprised recognition that God is at work in your life will make you, like Robert in the opening story of this chapter, excited that you are becoming a new person with a new identity.

Author's note: The scope of this book does not enable us to go into greater depth about our identity and the character of God. More study and more insights would be very helpful; therefore, I recommend two books with corresponding workbooks to aid your study: *The Search for Significance* and *Your Parents and You.*[2]

Questions

1. Before you read this chapter, what adjectives would you have used to describe yourself?

2. Which aspects of a codependent's identity apply to you? How has this identity influenced your life?

3. Paraphrase these passages:

   a)   Rom. 3:21-26

   b)   Col. 1:19-22

    c)   1 John 4:9-11

    d)   1 Cor. 6:19-20

    e)   Rom. 8:1

    f)   1 Pet. 2:9-10

    g)   2 Cor. 5:20

4. In what ways does your life (attitudes, thoughts, actions, relationships, etc.) reflect that you believe these passages? In what ways does your life indicate that you don't really believe them?

5. Describe your relationship with your parents (include both its positive and negative aspects):

6. How have these relationships affected your view of God?

7. Why have your attempts to try harder and please people more *not* given you a strong sense of worth?

8. Does the idea of "peeling the onion" in applying these truths encourage you or discourage you? Why?

9. Whom do you know (an individual or a group) that can help you in the healing process?

Eleven

Lordship: A Sense of Belonging

After a seminar at a weekend retreat in the Piney Woods of East Texas, I could tell that a young man looked troubled. As we walked outside, I asked, "James, what's the matter? Is something bothering you?"

"Yeah, it sure is!" Then turning to me, he said, "Can we take a walk? I want to ask you a question."

"Sure." We walked silently for a while until we were ambling down a path in the woods near a lake. "You have a question?" I asked.

James blurted out, "That last talk was about Christ being the Lord of our lives, giving us direction about what we should and shouldn't do. I can't buy that! I don't want Him to be the Lord of my life! Savior, okay—but not Lord."

"Why is that, James?"

"Life is hard enough now! Look at all the commands in the Bible! How can I do all of those when I'm already having a hard time keeping my life together?"

As we talked, I learned that James is a rescuer. He felt confused, angry, and guilty.

Codependent Fears About the Lordship of Christ

The lordship of Christ can be frightening for a codependent like James. Through the lenses of over-responsibility, perfectionism, repressed emotions, and guilt motivation, the beauty of an intimate relationship with Christ is distorted. Instead of a sense of belonging, trust, and affirmation, the codependent perceives the Christian message as one of more demands, more condemnation, and more guilt. Consequently, he feels driven and lonely.

Before we look at a picture of lordship, let's take a glance at several perspectives that many codependent believers have about Christ and the Christian life:

God is mean. Many of us do not believe that God has our best interests at heart. We think He only wants to use us. We may "serve" Him with many activities, but that service is done out of fear that He will punish us if we don't do exactly what He wants.

The Lord demands too much of me. Overly-responsible codependents fear that they can't measure up to the extremely high expectations of the Christian life. We are motivated by the double-edged sword of fear that we can't meet those expectations, and guilt that we have failed. We may give lip service to grace and forgiveness, but experience few of these freedoms and positive motivations.

I'm already trying as hard as I can, what more can I do? Similarly, the codependent feels anger, as well as guilt, at his perception of the demanding nature of God. Often, however, he channels his anger toward someone or some church or organization because he doesn't feel like he can be angry with God.

I don't want to lose control of my life. Living his life by controlling every detail, activity, and emotion, the codependent believer finds it extremely difficult to turn over that control to another person—even the Lord.

God will make me weird. Codependents are already lonely. They already feel strange and distant from others, and the stories of those who take a stand for Christ and suffer ridicule do not entice many to sign up!

I can gain worth by serving God. As a flip side to these perspectives, some codependents see Christian service as a means of gaining security and worth. Instead of backing away from a "radical" Christian commitment, these people plunge headlong into Christian activities in the hope of gaining recognition from others. Often, these people experience the same feelings of fear and guilt, but their thirst for approval drives them to take the risks of performing for acceptance.

If God loves me, He won't ask me to do anything hard. Codependents often read the Scriptures selectively, picking out passages that soothe, but overlooking passages that seem to feed their guilt motivation. As a reaction to the fear and guilt they have felt in their lives, some codependent believers focus entirely on one aspect of the character of God—His love—and can't see the balance of good motivations in the Scriptures.

The cumulative weight of some or all of these misguided perceptions is very destructive for believers who are in the grip of codependency. We make inaccurate conclusions about God (that He is demanding, harsh, or aloof) and about ourselves (that we can never measure up, or that we can gain a sense of worth by serving Him).

A Biblical Picture of Lordship

The Scriptures, however, present a very different picture of the lordship of Christ. One of the most helpful metaphors is of believers being bond-servants to God. Writers of the New Testament often used this idea to describe their relationship with Christ. Paul, James, and Peter each described himself as a *"bond-servant* of Jesus Christ" (Rom. 1:1; Phil. 1:1; Titus 1:1; James 1:1; and 2 Pet. 1:1). What does the term mean? And how can it help us to get a better picture of our relationship with the Lord?

Moses described it in Exodus 21:

> *Now these are the ordinances which you are to set before them. If you buy a Hebrew slave, he shall serve for six years; but on the seventh he shall go out as a free man without payment... But if the slave plainly says, " I love my master, my wife and my children; I will not go out as a free man," then his master shall bring him to God, then he shall bring him to the door or the doorpost. And his master shall pierce his ear with an awl; and he shall serve him permanently.*
>
> Ex. 21:1-2; 5-6

Becoming a bond-servant was based on two issues: the character of the master and a new identity of the slave. When it was time for the slave to be freed (verse two), the slave had a choice. If his master had been harsh, he could go free, but if he had experienced the love, protection, and provision of his master, he could choose to remain with him in a new relationship. The master would put a hole in the slave's ear, signifying to everyone that the slave had freely chosen to remain in the care of the master. At that point, the slave became a bondservant. His identity changed. His relationship with the master changed. His motivations changed. Instead of being *forced* to serve, he had *chosen* to serve. The love of the master compelled him to remain and to serve with joy, love, and respect. There existed "want-to," not "have-to" motivations based on the character of the master.

These twin motivations of love and respect are too often foreign to codependents. We may use these words, but we usually mean guilt and fear instead. As usual, we lean toward one of two extremes in our response to God (or our perception of Him). We tend to respond either in fear without love, or love without respect. This chart demonstrates these extremes as well as the balanced biblical motivations:

Fear without Love	Love and Respect (Biblical Fear)	Love without Respect
Condemnation, guilt, loneliness, withdrawal, or drivenness.	The love of God and the awesome character of God motivate us to know, love, obey, and serve Him.	It doesn't matter what we do; God still loves us, so we can do whatever we want to do.

As we have seen, the typical codependent responses to distortions about God result in fear, withdrawal, guilt, or drivenness to achieve a sense of worth or some combination of these. The biblical picture of being a bondservant, however, is based on a sense of belonging, a sense of being loved, and responding to the Master in affection and obedience because His character elicits both love and respect.

A Major Roadblock

Codependent Christians have a major roadblock that hinders their experience of the love and power of God. Many times in these pages we have seen how codependents try to get their sense of worth from rescuing, controlling, and serving others. We value the approval, the affection, and the respect of people because we have believed that their affirmation will give us the security and worth that we long for. We are guilty of the same sin that the Pharisees were. Jesus reproved them, *...for they loved the approval of men rather than the approval of God* (John 12:43). I don't mean to be too harsh, but we need to call this what it is: *idolatry.*

Any time a person tries to get his security and value from someone or something other than the Lord, it is idolatry. When we attempt to control other people or to secure power and approval by serving, we are putting ourselves in God's place. The surrender of manipulative control and the acceptance of God's grace are central to the Christian faith,[1] but as we have seen, the codependent usually tries to control his own life and the lives of others. He doesn't want to give up control; he wants more control. Almost as a truism of codependency, codependents serve to control, gain power and approval. Therefore, that service is idolatrous.

"Wait a minute!" someone might say. "What about Jesus? The Bible says that He came to serve. Was He codependent? Was His service idolatrous?"

Yes, Jesus did, in fact, serve. He served more than anyone ever has or ever will, but He was definitely not codependent. He offered His help, but He let people make their own decisions. He let them walk away, and at one point all of the multitude, except for the twelve disciples, abandoned Him. He spoke the truth and let people respond however they chose. In the garden of Gethsemane, He was completely objective about His ordeal of suffering. He didn't repress His emotions. Even when He was abandoned by the twelve, he continued to do the Father's will.

There are two dominant motivations to serve: one is to gain a sense of worth. That is idolatry. The other motivation is entirely different. It is serving out of appreciation for God's grace and your worth in Him. The first motivation results in fear, guilt, withdrawal, and drivenness. The second results in love, trust, and joyful obedience.

As codependents, we have been following the wrong master! We have served a compulsive spouse, a nagging parent, a critical and condemning friend in the vain hope of gaining approval. These masters are not benevolent, but we keep serving them. We learn to tolerate criticism and live with fear and guilt because we think this is normal. We believe we are bad people, and that we deserve to be treated that way. As Melanie Beattie observes:

> Not only do many of us begin tolerating abnormal, unhealthy, and inappropriate behaviors, we take it one step further: we convince ourselves these behaviors are normal and what we deserve. We may become so familiar with verbal abuse and

disrespectful treatment that we don't even recognize when these things are happening. But deep inside, an important part of us knows. [2]

As you recognize your propensity to gain your sense of worth by pleasing people (especially that *certain* person), you may be overwhelmed with the depth of that tendency in your life. It may seem impossible to change. But hang in there! Objectivity is often painful, but the Lord is a kind and patient Master. He knows your past and He knows your pain. Instead of seeing Him as a demanding God that you can never please, learn to see Him as a kind and gentle Father who will give you all the encouragement, strength, and time you need. Overcoming a lifetime of idolatry is tough, but it is possible. You can be free! As your identity and your view of God begin to change, you will have an increasing sense that God does indeed care about you deeply, that He is trustworthy, and that He has a wonderful plan for your life.

Questions

1. Are you afraid of Christ becoming the Master of your life? If so, why? How do you normally respond to Him?

2. How would responding to the Lord as His *bond-servant* change your relationship with God and your service for Him?

3. Describe ways that rescuing and controlling are idolatrous:

4. Describe ways that you either withdraw from others in fear or are driven to serve them to prove your worth:

5. What are some ways an idolater can be transformed into a bond-servant? Be specific:

6. Picture in your mind the process of the transformation mentioned in the preceding question. As you visualize that process, describe what you see:

Twelve

Find a Friend

Originally, I had planned to put this chapter toward the end of the book. Then I decided that it ought to be placed earlier in the flow, somewhere in the middle or maybe at the beginning of Part 3, "The Process." The more I thought about it, however, the more it seemed that the relational aspect of emerging from the eclipse of codependency should have a more prominent position. So here it is, very early in the explanation of "The Solution"! The reasons for this prominent place will hopefully become obvious within the next few pages.

You cannot overcome the grip of codependency alone. You may learn some good information. You may be able to apply some of what you learn at a certain level of your life, but there is too much deception and too little objectivity within us to fight the battle alone. Our thought patterns are too ingrained and our habits too well established. We need the honesty and encouragement of someone else to make substantial progress. We need to see someone model what it means to gain our self-worth from the Lord and experience the freedom and motivation of the Christian life.

This kind of friendship is rare, but there are people (some of whom you may not yet know) who can provide this environment for your growth. Do not look for another codependent who needs you to need him! Don't look for someone to rescue you! Instead, look for someone who will affirm you, encourage you, be honest with you, and be a good model for you.

The Lord never intended for any of His people to try to make it as "Lone Ranger Christians." Scripture gives numerous admonitions and descriptions regarding relationships among believers. Paul encouraged the believers at Ephesus to use their spiritual gifts to benefit one another:

> *...until we all attain to the unity of the faith, and of the knowledge of the Son of God, to a mature man, to the measure of the stature which belongs to the fulness of Christ. As a result, we are no longer to be children, tossed here and there by waves, and carried about by every wind of doctrine, by the trickery of men, by craftiness in deceitful scheming; but speaking the truth in love, we are to grow up in all aspects into Him, who is the head, even Christ, from whom the whole body, being fitted and held together by that which every joint supplies, according to the proper working of each individual part, causes the growth of the body for the building up of itself in love.* Eph. 4:13-16

Every Christian has a role to play in the lives of other believers. We are all part of the body of Christ, giving and receiving encouragement and strength from one another.

Similarly, the writer to the Hebrews instructed them:

> *...and let us consider how to stimulate one another to love and good deeds, not forsaking our own assembling together, as is the habit of some, but encouraging one another; and all the more, as you see the day drawing near.*
>
> Heb. 10:24-25

So then, finding people to encourage us is not only practical, it is also a biblical instruction. We need each other, but sadly, some of us are quite reticent to find a friend.

Doug is a young man with a painful past. When he learned about the effects of drug addiction in his family, some of his repressed hurt and anger began to submerge. Frank is a friend of Doug's who really wanted to help him, and as he found out a little about Doug's pain, he began to ask questions to help draw him out a little more. But Doug began to withdraw instead of opening up, so Frank told him, "Doug, I'll be glad to talk to you about your family anytime you want to talk, but it doesn't seem like you want to right now. Is that right?"

"Yeah," Doug said. "I guess I don't want to think about it now. Maybe later."

The days and weeks went by, and after several months, Frank told Doug, "Hey, I know you don't want to talk about your past, but you really ought to find somebody to talk to. That kind of thing can destroy a person!"

"I know you're right," Doug said. "I do need to talk about it, and I will, but not right now."

Frank didn't think he was getting very far, but he knew if he pressed it, Doug would never open up. He told Doug, "Okay, Bud. That's fine. I'm here when you need me."

"Thanks, Frank."

It was a perfect situation. Doug needed a friend, and Frank was about as sensitive and kind as anyone could be. But Doug still wouldn't discuss his pain with him. Perhaps he was afraid that if all of his hurt and anger were exposed, he would be overwhelmed. Perhaps he thought that if Frank really knew what was inside him, Frank would reject him. He couldn't take that.

Another person had a better response. Lisa had been married to an alcoholic for twelve years. They had divorced, leaving her with two sons to raise alone. The difficulties of getting a job and being a single parent were compounded by a backlog of pain produced by her codependency. She tried to cope. She tried to organize her life and control her boys, but after a while, her life began to come apart at the seams. A friend from church said to her, "Lisa, why don't you go see Rob Johnston at the church? I heard from somebody that he understands situations like yours. He's a kind man. See if he can help you."

Lisa made an appointment with Rob. He listened patiently as she tried to explain the jumbled mosaic of both what had happened to her and how she felt about it. He took some time to explain how alcoholism affects the whole family. Lisa couldn't believe what she was hearing! Rob was describing her thoughts and feelings exactly!

"How did you know what I've been thinking? Have you been reading my mail?" Lisa was both surprised and amused by Rob's understanding.

Rob smiled and replied, "No, I haven't been reading your mail. These are the attitudes and actions that seem to be common in people from dysfunctional families. You seem to relate to them pretty well."

Rob then explained that a group of people with similar backgrounds met every Thursday night to talk about their problems and to give support to each other.

"Would you like to come?" he asked.

Lisa was hesitant. "Well, who comes to these meetings?" Lisa was afraid that these people would think she was weird and crazy.

"I'll be there, and a lot of other people in our church and in the community come, too," Rob reassured her.

"Okay," she said haltingly. "I'll be there."

Lisa thought of a hundred excuses not to go on Thursday night, but she mustered the courage to ask a neighbor to look out for the boys, then she got in her car and drove to the church. When she walked in the door, several people she knew greeted her! "What are you doing here?!?" she blurted out without thinking.

Someone laughed and said, "The same thing you're here for!" They both laughed.

For the next hour, and for the next several months, Lisa felt understood and encouraged. She gained new insights about her identity, her relationship with her husband, the rest of her family, and practically everything else in her life. She had found an environment of loving relationships. The process had many ups and downs, but she began to experience healing as she found herself in relationships which provided affirmation, encouragement, honesty, and positive examples to follow.

Affirmation

God's love and acceptance of us is based on His grace, not on our goodness or good deeds to win His approval. Throughout the Scriptures, our identity is explained in terms of who we are. What we do is a response to that identity. A classic passage of this response to our identity is found in Peter's first letter. He wrote:

> *But you are a chosen race, a royal priesthood, a holy nation,*
> *a people for God's own possession, that you may proclaim the*
> *excellencies of Him who has called you out of darkness into*
> *His marvelous light.*   1 Pet. 2:9

It is fine to tell people that their performance is good, but it is much better to affirm people for who they are. One woman remarked that her new boss took time to listen to her and then expressed confidence in her because of her maturity and integrity. When she tried to impress him with her great ideas about the job, he responded, "Those are excellent ideas. Just be yourself and everything will be great." That affirmation freed her to be honest, bold, and creative.

But what about the times we fail? That's when the chips are down in relationships. That's when we see if people are truly affirming or demanding. That's when my friend, Melanie Ahlquist, is at her best. For several years, Melanie has been the Associate Regional Director in the South for Campus Crusade for Christ. She has had the opportunity to see lots of people in all kinds of situations. When people do well, Melanie rejoices with them. That's not so unusual. But when they fail, Melanie looks them squarely in the eye and tells them gently, but convincingly:

"It's okay. That hasn't changed how I feel about you at all. I care about you, and there's nothing you can do to keep me from caring about you!" The pain of failure and the fear of rejection seem to dissolve in the presence of that kind of affirmation. (When you're feeling down, just call Melanie. Her phone number is...Just kidding, Mel!)

Codependents who have obtained their identity only from their ability to perform and please people (and come up short!) sometimes have a difficult time believing that they can be accepted for just who they are. It may take a while to believe and experience that kind of affirmation, but it is vitally important to growth and development.

Encouragement

A spirit of encouragement is closely linked to affirmation. This is like a coach on the sideline, cheering on his players. "You can do it! Don't stop now! Cut to the left! Now pass the ball!" He gives directions as he communicates confidence in the players. Over the course of a season or two, the players develop both skill and confidence that they can execute the plays needed to win.

I have several people who play that role in my life, but none as much as my wife, Joyce. Whenever I am discouraged, she communicates confidence in me. Whenever I need some fresh ideas, she usually has plenty of them. When I'm heading in a new direction, she asks me questions that I haven't even thought of, so that I can be more aware of opportunities and pitfalls. Whenever I need someone to believe in me, she is there.

All of us need somebody, or several somebodies, to give us that combination of direction, feedback, and confidence.

Honesty

Most of us have repressed deep hurts and anger for years. These emotions surface from time to time, but not in healthy, constructive ways. We get depressed for weeks, or we explode in anger over something relatively small. We need a friend who will let us express our emotions and thoughts in a safe environment, without fear of being ridiculed for feeling and thinking the way we do. We need people who won't give us simple answers, like "Just pray about it," or "Boy, you need to confess that and move on," or "Give thanks in all things, then don't think about it again." These may be well-meaning admonitions, but they only encourage more repression.

Exposing our cumulative hurt and anger is usually a very messy process. As Todd began to see how his parents' divorce had made him an overly-responsible rescuer, he determined to stop rescuing his mother. It didn't quite work out that neatly, however. I saw him recently, and he told me about his last encounter with his mother. He was angry. "I saw it coming—the self-pity, the threat of rejection—and I didn't want to rescue her, but I did it again!" Todd's honesty gave us a chance to talk about the situation.

We also need a patient listener who, after hearing us, will then be honest with us. In our lack of objectivity, we may come to wrong conclusions. A friend might tell you, "No, I don't think that's the way to respond to your husband. That is rescuing him again. You need to let him be responsible for his own choices and experience the consequences, too." Truth can be communicated quickly, but love and grace are not so quickly learned, especially by people who have seldom experienced them.

Honesty in relationships works both ways. You need someone you can talk to without fear of ridicule or gossip about your life. And you also need someone who will be honest, sometimes painfully honest, with you.

Modeling

Reading books, going to classes, and listening to tapes can be helpful, but people's lives are changed most by seeing an example. As in every other aspect of life, emotional and spiritual health is "caught, not taught." Codependents need to spend time with healthy people in healthy situations where real emotions are expressed and real solutions are found to real problems. Phonyness and superficial answers won't cut it!

We need to observe these people as they respond to their own successes and failures, and those of others. And we need to see them in as many different situations as possible: job, family, recreation, church, etc. This is the same pattern that Christ established in His relationship with His disciples. They were with Him almost constantly for more than three years. They observed Him in the good times: healing the sick, giving sight to the blind, raising the dead, and speaking to the multitudes at the height of His popularity. They must have had incredible discussions as they walked along and sat around the campfires so many times together. They also saw Christ respond to hard-hearted legalists as they condemned Him. They saw Him experience ridicule, and they observed Him weep at unbelief and death. They watched Him agonize in prayer over His impending torture and execution. And finally, they saw the risen Christ in His glory before He ascended into the clouds from a hilltop outside Jerusalem. They saw Him in every conceivable situation!

Obviously, we don't have any models like that! But there are people we can watch and learn from, people who are honest about the struggle of life and faithful to believe God in the midst of that struggle. Joyce points to Ann Dahl, her college group leader for Campus Crusade for Christ, as the person who modeled the reality of the Christian life at a pivotal point in her life. She reflects: "What I remember most about Ann is seeing her trust God in all kinds of situations. Some were good. Some were bad. Some were easy, some were hard. She didn't have simple answers all the time. She was real. It was a time in my life when I really needed a good example to follow, and Ann was there!"

We all need people like Ann at critical points in our lives—like when we're trying to come to grips with our codependency!

But Who?

Okay, you say, *so I need someone who will affirm and encourage me, be honest with me, and model a real and healthy life. But who?* Good question! You may already know someone who can help you, or it may take some looking. You may not know anybody right now who can be that kind of friend. For some of us, our spouses are a major part of the problems we are experiencing, but for others (myself included), our spouses can provide the understanding and patience we need to help us heal and grow.

A pastor can probably help you find a friend, or he may direct you to a group that discusses codependency and emotional health. Or you may want to find a qualified Christian counselor to help you. The person you select will be determined by a number of factors, including their availability and schedule, and your desire. You may want the professional care and confidentiality of a counselor, but be sure that you find one whose counseling is based on biblical principles.

There is a stigma about counseling in the minds of some people. They believe that "all counselors are quacks," and that you have to be "really messed up" to go to one. Not everybody needs to go to a counselor, but many people would benefit from the warmth, affirmation, and objectivity that a good counselor can provide.

The grip of codependency is strong. We cannot make it on our own, so find a friend to help you.

Questions

1. What might or might not happen if you try to deal with your codependency alone?

2. How can a friend, group, or counselor help you? Be specific.

3. Make a list of people, groups, and qualified counselors you can select from. Which of these is best for you? Why?

Thirteen

Three Ingredients:

No. 1: Identify

As a codependent learns more about how he has been affected by dysfunctional relationships, he also learns how to respond in new and more positive ways. These new responses are characterized by three essential ingredients: identify, detach, and decide. First, he can *identify* the behaviors, feelings, thoughts, words, and actions that have become the habits of codependency. Then he can *detach* and reflect about the situation, how he can stop responding in the usual way, and instead respond in a positive, healthy way. After that reflection, he can *decide* on his course of action. It will be a response based on objective reality, not a reaction based on codependent reflexes.

Identify. Detach. Decide. See it. Analyze it. Choose your response. This is the path to freedom and health, and in these next three chapters, we will examine these three ingredients. First, we will see how we can *identify* our codependent behaviors.

A few months ago, I watched the movie *Ben Hur*. (This is the second *Ben Hur* illustration in this book. Can you tell that I like this movie?) Toward the end of the movie is a poignant scene. Judah Ben Hur has just left his mother and sister in the valley of the lepers. He blames himself for their fate. He is crushed, heart-broken, and bitter over their predicament. He staggers back to the now run-down family estate, crosses the courtyard, and sees Esther, his love of years past before calamity struck the family. Would they renew their relationship? Would Esther comfort Judah?

Judah, too bitter and full of self-pity to express affection, said sadly, "I would love you, but I would only destroy you like I've destroyed the others."

Esther recognized that Judah had changed from the strong, confident, loving man she had known before. "I loved Judah Ben Hur," she said resolutely, looking into his eyes. "But you're not that man! I've lost you, Judah." And she walked out, leaving Judah in his self-pity.

As I watched that scene, a realization struck me. Esther didn't try to rescue him! She let him make his own choices! She was objective and independent. She was not codependent!

As we learn more about our identity in Christ, and as we see the patterns of codependency in our lives, we will be able to identify many of the specific codependent things we say and do. Also, we'll be able to see some specific characteristics of codependency in others. For some, identifying codependent behavior will be fairly easy: *Oh yeah! I've done that for years!* Others will have a harder time identifying those behaviors. People like this may see a few instances, but they don't see the patterns of codependency very clearly. Still others lack objectivity to such an extent that they don't see any characteristics of their codependency at all. They just don't get the picture, and healing can't begin until the Holy Spirit begins to overcome their denial.

Identifying codependent behavior is the trigger mechanism for objective reflection, and for ultimately living in freedom and godly independence. Before this realization begins, however, most of us think that our situations are normal.

What Is "Normal"?

Dysfunctional behavior destroys objectivity. As a result, codependents believe their lives are fairly normal. If we compare our lives to that of the alcoholic, drug addict, perfectionist, workaholic, bulimic, sexual abuser, or whoever in the family is "really messed up," we think we're doing pretty well. We fail to recognize that exaggeration, guilt, loneliness, being manipulated, manipulating others, and outbursts of anger are signs of relational pathology, not normalcy. But we are unable to see the devastation in our own lives (which are not "normal") because of our inability to face reality.

What is reality? Most codependents have a difficult time with it. Many of us believe that we are terrible people (though we try so hard to help), and that the offending person in our lives is wonderful (though he manipulates us through guilt, self-pity, anger, and fear).

Other codependents rationalize that they are very good people with no wrong motives or hidden faults. The strength of this deception is so great that at one point, a young man I know told me that he didn't think he had ever sinned. Yet at other times in his life, this same man was overcome with guilt and morbid introspection. Fairly black-and-white, don't you think?

Codependents are the products of dysfunctional families. These families are not normal, but are pathological to one degree or another. Most of us have defended and rescued the people in our lives so much that we have never seen the truth about them, and the truth can be difficult to swallow.

One woman I know had defended her alcoholic mother all her life. As she learned about her codependency, she remarked with surprise, "I've always thought that she was normal, but now I'm starting to see that her praise and condemnation have been designed to manipulate me so that I would please her and rescue her. She isn't normal. She's sick!"

Our responses haven't been normal either. We have felt guilty even when we've tried to help. We have felt lonely when we wanted intimacy so badly. We have controlled, been controlled, and rescued people from the consequences of their choices. We haven't allowed ourselves to feel normal hurt and normal anger when these people have condemned, used, and ignored us. We haven't been "normal" at all!

Reality demands that we open our eyes to the truth (the good and the bad), recognize the evil in all people (even ourselves), and realize that life is a struggle. Blindness never helps in the long run.

Red Flags

Throughout these pages, we have looked at many examples of codependent behavior. These should serve as red flags for us. *That's me; that's what I do!* or *My wife does that to me!* or *I respond that way to my husband.* Some of us see a few particular events, but don't see any deep-rooted patterns in our behavior. One man told me about his relationship with his condemning, manipulative father. "I've been angry with my father several times, so I guess I'm pretty objective," he surmised. He didn't see the pervasive insecurity and myriad of defense mechanisms that he had developed during his life. We need to see both the patterns and the specific events that make up those patterns.

At the risk of being redundant, we will list some of the more common codependent feelings and behaviors. For simplicity, we will divide these by the savior and Judas categories. Which of these, or variations of these, can you identify in your life?

Savior	Judas
Feelings:	**Feelings:**
grandiose importance, superior, certain, euphoric, confident, appreciated, angry, self-righteous, jealous, possessive, easily hurt	depressed, lonely, angry, helpless, confused, fear, hurt, inferior, hopeless, guilt, numbness, trapped, martyr, persecuted, lethargic, worthless, shame, tired
Thoughts and Words:	**Thoughts and Words:**
It's all your fault. *You made me fail.* *I can help.* *He (she) needs me.* *Why aren't people as perceptive as I am?* *I deserve their respect and love.* *I can make life good.*	*It's all my fault.* *I'm a failure.* *I can't do anything right.* *Everything I do is wrong.* *Yes,* but I mean *no.* *No,* but I mean *yes.* *I don't deserve their respect and love.* *Life will never be good for me.*
Black or White:	**Black or White:**
People really need me. *I am indispensable to the kingdom of God.* *People won't be helped and the Great Commission can't be fulfilled without me.*	*People really need me, but I'll only let them down.* *Good Christians wouldn't think or act this way.* *God must be mad at me. He'll punish me.*
Actions:	**Actions:**
exaggerate (high), self-promotion, overcommitted, workaholism, easily manipulated, control others through praise and condemnation, rescue people without being asked, deny reality, compulsion to avoid failure, giving, helping, try to please people, defensive, overly responsible, outbursts of anger, rationalizes, trusts self and others	exaggerate (low), self-denigration, withdrawal, avoid people and risks, easily manipulated, control others through self-pity, deny reality, passive-aggressive, afraid to fail, believes he can't please anybody, defensive, irresponsible, outbursts of anger, rationalizes, doesn't trust self but may trust others

As we have seen, a person can experience the symptoms of a "savior" at one moment and the characteristics of a "Judas" the next. Take a few minutes to circle the feelings, thoughts, words, and actions that characterize your life to a significant degree. Is there a pattern?

Identifying codependent behavior may seem like a very cognitive exercise, but it usually elicits a flood of emotions as we realize how deeply we have been affected. There is both good and bad news in this realization. The good news is: There is hope! The Lord can give us wisdom and strength, and a friend can give us the encouragement we need to fight our battles. The bad news is: What you see is probably only the first layer of the onion. As you deal with the hurts, fears, anger, and habits there, yet another layer will be exposed. Is that discouraging to you? It probably is, but this is reality, and we need to face reality no matter how difficult it is. Remember, you are not alone. The Lord will give you the grace to endure and progress. Paul encouraged the believers in Corinth:

> *No temptation has overtaken you but such as is common to man; and God is faithful, who will not allow you to be tempted beyond what you are able, but with the temptation will provide the way of escape also, that you may be able to endure it.*　　　　1 Cor. 10:13

The way of escape so that we may endure begins when we *identify* our codependent behavior, then *detach* and reflect on reality, and finally, *decide* on the best course of action.

Questions

1. Have you thought of your family as "normal"? Is it? Why, or why not?

2. Take some time to identify codependent behavior in your life. Be as specific as possible as you describe your feelings, thoughts, statements, and actions.

Savior

    a) Feelings:

    b) Thoughts and words:

    c) Actions:

Judas

    a) Feelings:

b) Thoughts and words:

c) Actions:

3. List four specific situations when you responded with codependent behavior. Then describe each one. Describe what a healthy, non-codependent response would look like in each of these situations.

Situation 1:

a) Codependent response:

b) Feelings:

c) Thoughts and words:

d) Actions:

e) Healthy response:

Situation 2:

a) Codependent response:

b) Feelings:

c) Thoughts and words:

d) Actions:

e) Healthy response:

Situation 3:

a) Codependent response:

b) Feelings:

c) Thoughts and words:

d) Actions:

e) Healthy response:

Situation 4:

a) Codependent response:

b) Feelings:

c) Thoughts and words:

d) Actions:

e) Healthy response:

Fourteen

Three Ingredients:

No. 2: Detach

When Joyce and I bought our house in Austin several years ago, we had to plant our lawn, shrubs, and everything else in the yard. The tree in the front yard (in Central Texas, it is a great privilege to have *a* tree in the yard!) was in a slightly peculiar position. Its roots were a little exposed on the downhill side, so I decided to build a rock wall around that side with the rocks left over from building the house.

It was my first attempt at masonry. I bought some cement and sand, and had planned to buy a trowel until I learned it would cost almost seven dollars. That seemed too steep a price to pay for such a small job, so I passed on the trowel.

I mixed the cement in a big trash can and proceeded to lay the rock and cement, smoothing the mortar with my hands. Three hours later, I had almost finished the wall. It was a lot harder than I had thought it would be!

For twenty or thirty minutes during this time, I had noticed a tingling sensation in my fingers, but thought it was just because my hands had been wet for so long. I washed off my hands with the hose, and was shocked to see that the skin on the ends of my fingers was gone in several places! There were deep holes! I quickly finished the wall and went into the house to see the extent of the damage. It was, I learned, a case of concrete poisoning.

I had to put antibiotic cream and band-aids on the ends of my fingers for almost two weeks, and today there are scars on those fingers. One of the amazing things about this incident is that there was so little warning, so little sense of "something's wrong!" Only when the wounds were exposed was there a realization of the damage. Then healing could begin.

That story is analogous to codependency. When we finally observe the damage that has occurred in our lives, we may be shocked by its extensiveness. It takes time and attention for healing to transpire. We need to identify that damage, reflect on the best course of action, and take steps toward healing: identify, detach, and decide. This chapter is about detachment.

The Need to Detach

Codependents are trained to react, not respond. We instinctively rescue, withdraw, or attack. We feel the compassion of a rescuer, and we feel anger, hurt, and self-pity. This instinct is deeply ingrained in us, but it needs to be changed. We need to detach; to separate ourselves from that codependent reaction system, and think, feel, and reflect.

Jill invited her mother for a visit. She cleaned the house, planned the week, and got her guest room in perfect shape. Soon after her mother arrived, however, she started making some "subtle" hints to Jill. "So, I see you still have those curtains." "It *is* hard to get dishes like that really clean, isn't it?" "Is that the same dress I gave you seven years ago?" "Oh, I'll just have to give you *my* recipe for this sometime!"

Jill's feelings of guilt and shame mounted with each comment. Then she realized what was happening. She had been learning about her codependency, and this was a classic example. Jill went to her bedroom, sat down, and wrote down how she felt and how she had responded to her mother. She realized that she didn't have to agree with her mother's insinuations about her house, her cooking, her clothes, or herself. She spent some time reflecting on the contrast between her codependent identity (*I'm a bad person*, etc.) and her identity in Christ (unconditionally loved, forgiven, accepted, secure, etc.), and went back into the living room with a new sense of confidence. During the next several days of her mother's visit, Jill had to detach quite a few times to gain a proper perspective of her identity. Sometimes she didn't do this quickly enough, but overall, Jill began to develop a habit of detaching.

Detachment requires time, objectivity, and distance (emotionally, physically, or both). Circumstances vary so widely that there cannot be a formula for detaching, but there is a question that can help you: *What do I need* (time, space, objectivity) *so that I can reflect on this situation?*

Sometimes we can identify, detach, and decide in a heartbeat. This is especially true when we've had ample practice in this process. Many times, however, we need to remove ourselves from the offending person or situation to be more objective. The pressure of close proximity is simply too strong. Go to another room, take a drive in the country (under the speed limit!), go away for a weekend. Do whatever you need to do so that you can feel and think. A distraction may help you gain a sense of calm before you reflect. Read a book or magazine, watch a television show, take a walk. Do whatever helps you.

Some psychologists use *detach* to describe the act of isolating oneself from others in a negative, harmful way. In contrast, codependent literature uses the word to describe a positive healthy action: stepping back to obtain objectivity about a person or situation. Therefore, detachment is not the same as withdrawal, though it may appear to be at first. Withdrawal is a defensive reaction to block pain and avoid reality. Detachment has the opposite goal: to become objective, deal with reality, feel real emotions, and determine the best course of action.

The Scriptures have a lot to say about reflecting on reality and truth so that we can respond wisely instead of reacting codependently. We are instructed to take time to acquire this wisdom:

> *Acquire wisdom! Acquire understanding! Do not forget, nor turn away from the words of my mouth. Do not forsake her,*

*and she will guard you; love her, and she will watch over
you. The beginning of wisdom is: Acquire wisdom; and with
all your acquiring, get understanding.*

Prov. 4:5-7

As we have seen in a previous chapter, a friend can sometimes be
instrumental in helping us feel pain and be objective.

*By wisdom a house is built, and by understanding it is
established; and by knowledge the rooms are filled with all
precious and pleasant riches. A wise man is strong, and a
man of knowledge increases power. For by wise guidance
you will wage war, and in abundance of counselors there is
victory.*   Prov. 24:3-6

And we can learn how to respond to people who condemn, neglect,
and manipulate us:

*Do not answer a fool according to his folly, lest you also be
like him. Answer a fool as his folly deserves, lest he be wise
in his own eyes.*   Prov. 26:4-5

These are just a sampling of the rich instructions offered in the
Scriptures about detaching and reflecting.

Aids for Detaching

As you learn to detach so that you can be honest about your feelings
and objective about your circumstances, you will see a sharpening
contrast between codependent and healthy thoughts, feelings, and actions.
Perhaps it would be helpful to list some questions to ask yourself when
you detach. These are some suggestions:

- *Why did he (she) say (do) that to me?*
- *What did he (she) mean?*
- *How do I feel about it?*
- *How would a healthy person feel?*
- *Is he (she) controlling me? Condemning me? Neglecting me?*
- *Why do I feel guilty? Driven? Afraid? Lonely?*
- *Am I rescuing?*
- *Am I acting as a savior? A Judas?*

Also, it might be helpful to develop some statements that trigger certain thought processes in your mind. This may seem "hokey," but getting a handle on objectivity is very difficult for codependents. Use whatever helps you! Here are a few statements that may help you think and feel:

- *I'm not responsible for making him (her) happy.*
- *I'm not responsible for fixing the problem.*
- *He (she) needs to be responsible for himself (herself).*
- *I can respond calmly.*
- *I can say no.*
- *I can say yes.*
- *I can make my own decisions.*
- *I feel angry...lonely...guilty...driven...afraid.*
- *I am loved, forgiven, and accepted by God through Jesus Christ.*

It is also a good idea to memorize some of the passages of Scripture that we looked at in chapter 10 about our identity in Christ.

These questions and statements, and those that seem to fit your personality and situations, will help you in your efforts to detach, feel, and reflect. As you detach, consider the following:

Your Options

Codependents are accustomed to limited options. We usually react by rescuing, helping, withdrawing, attacking, or by whatever else we have learned instinctively. If we change our response, we tend to feel awkward and guilty. That's why it's so important to detach. Then we can see the contrast between codependent reactions and healthy responses. When we become convinced that healthy responses are indeed healthy, we will gradually feel less awkward as we try them.

Detaching is a bit like being in a small boat that is cut loose from an ocean liner going in the wrong direction. There may be a certain sense of safety in being tied to the giant liner, but it isn't going where you want to go. You cut the lines and suddenly you're on your own, drifting in the open ocean. It feels awkward. You are confused and afraid. Soon, you begin to make some halting attempts to navigate. You make a few wrong moves, but you make a few right ones, too. You begin moving in the direction you want to go. With experience and practice, your confidence grows and your independence transitions from awkward fright to exhilaration.

In the same way, detaching is a way to "cut the ropes" of codependency, but most of us, in our early attempts, feel awkward, confused, and afraid. We need to get out our navigational charts and sailing books to examine our options.

Soon we will be able to anticipate our need to detach, and we can practice "prevenient detachment." *Prevenient* means "to come before; to anticipate." Prevenient detachment means to think through the situation before it happens. Learn to think, reflect, ask questions, and be prepared for situations before they occur. Someone might think that considering a situation before it occurs is harmful introspection and vain imagining, but there is a tremendous difference between prevenient detachment and vain thoughts. Vain thoughts are based on codependent, black-or-white hopes and fears. They are not objective. Prevenient detachment is based on objectivity and truth, not unrealistic hopes and fears. One results in more blindness, more unreality, and more codependent behavior. The other results in preparation, objective reality, and productive steps of progress.

It is a binary trap to assume that there are only two options: either continue reacting in the same way that you have before, or stop reacting that way. It's true that you can stop, but there are usually many other options to choose from. Take some time to list some of the many possibilities. If you can anticipate awkward situations, contemplate your possible responses. To prod your thinking, ask questions like:

- *What are realistic expectations? How does he/she usually respond to me?*
- *What do I want from this conversation* (visit, encounter, etc.)?
- *What if I do this: _____?*
- *What if I do that: _____?*
- *How can I respond if this or that happens?*

In the previous example of Jill's mother's visit, Jill detached by going into her bedroom on several occasions to reflect, feel, and think clearly. Several of those times, she wrote about her present thoughts and emotions by using some of the questions and statements in this chapter. Then she thought about the various ways she could respond to her mother. She could try to ignore her. (She had tried that before.) She could repress the hurt and anger until she blew up at her mother. (That had happened a few times, too.) She could tell her mother off, condemning her for all the nit-picky comments she could think of. Or, she could determine to ignore some of it, but calmly and firmly take a stand on certain things.

That predetermined plan enabled Jill to be in control of her own emotions, thoughts, and words, instead of being controlled by her mother. When they disagreed a few times, she could see that her mother didn't appreciate her honesty. So with fresh maternal condemnation, Jill again detached at an appropriate time, going to her bedroom to regroup. Over the course of the visit, Jill gradually developed a new habit of identifying the way she usually reacted to her mother, detaching to feel and reflect, and then deciding on a healthy, independent course of action.

Some Perspectives on Detaching

Charting a new course for a specific situation or for a lifetime can be very awkward and frightening. There are so many changes, so many emotions, and seemingly, so little time. These are some perspectives on the process of detaching:

Detaching in love or anger

It is best to detach calmly and with a loving attitude, but that isn't always possible. It may seem harsh or selfish to put such a premium on detachment, but being controlled by someone and pleasing him above all else is *not* a good thing. It is idolatry. If you have the choice either to detach in anger or in love, by all means do it in love. But by *all* means, detach. Melody Beattie wrote:

> *I think it is better to do everything in an attitude of love.*
> *However, for a variety of reasons, we can't always do that. If*
> *you can't detach in love, it's my opinion that it is better to detach*
> *in anger rather to stay attached. If we are detached, we are in a*
> *better position to work on (or through) our resentful emotions.*
> *If we're attached, we probably won't do anything other than stay*
> *upset.* [1]

Anger can actually be used constructively in the process of detaching. It is a strong motivation to develop your independence and identity. Constructive anger can be seen in thoughts like: *I refuse to be manipulated again*, or *I'm not going to take this anymore. I'm going to detach so I can develop my own identity and make my own decisions.*

Detaching perfectly

Some of us are such obsessive–compulsive perfectionists that we think we have to do everything perfectly when we detach! One woman told me that she was afraid to detach because she "might not do it just right, and what would my father say if I made a mistake?" After a few minutes, she realized that this perfectionism and fear were the very reasons she needed to detach!

A young man who was learning to detach came to a startling realization. He was driven to succeed and to always "be right," but one day, as he sat in a sales meeting, the thought hit him, *I don't* have *to be right*. He did not instantly become irresponsible, but instead, became more bold and confident as he developed the habit of detaching.

If we believe that we have to say and do everything perfectly when we detach, then we are still carrying an oppressive weight of responsibility. Be realistic. Detaching requires a major change in thoughts, feelings, and emotions. Changes like these are not computerized. We are not robots. We are people, and people need time, practice, and patience to change deeply ingrained habits.

How would a "normal" person respond?

Drawing a comparison between our codependent reactions and the healthy responses of a "normal" person is very instructive. Some of us, however, may recoil at this thought because our perception is: Codependent people are giving and loving; "normal" people are selfish and prideful. That perception demonstrates a continued lack of objectivity about codependency. It still sees the virtue in rescuing without seeing its hidden selfishness and idolatry.

It is true that "normal" people, like all of us, are sinners who are prone to selfishness and pride, but for our purposes we are using *normal* to mean simply non-codependent and independent. A healthy, independent person may seem terribly selfish because he isn't controlled by the whims of others, but we don't need to label him as a terrible, awful, no good, very bad person because he makes his own decisions.

Expect conflict

When you stop playing a codependent role in your family, don't expect everybody to applaud you for your growth and development! They have lived their lives by having you rescue them as they controlled you. As they realize that you are no longer controllable, they may step up the pressure. They may use stronger manipulation: more guilt, more condemnation, and more withdrawal. They may be accusing: "You are so selfish!"

When you stop playing your codependent role in the family, expect conflict; expect to be isolated from the family. As the family reforms its boundaries, family members may leave you on the outside. The fear of this isolation is the motivation that often compels codependents to continue to be used, neglected, and controlled. It takes both objectivity and courage to take these bold and necessary steps.

Freedom, confusion, and pain

In our era of advanced technology, change comes with the push of a button. But people aren't machines. We don't make major changes quickly and effortlessly. The process of identifying, detaching, and deciding produces a hodge-podge of conflicting emotions and thoughts. Like being cut free from the ocean liner that is going in the wrong direction, we have a new sense of freedom and independence. But with that freedom comes the pain of realizing how codependency has damaged your life and the confusion of not being confident and secure in your new direction.

Don't despair if you feel awkward and afraid as you learn to detach. These feelings are simply a part of the reality of change. Accept them for now. They will gradually abate as your confidence grows. You will increasingly enjoy your independence and freedom.

Is divorce a good option?

For some, the pain and bitterness of their marriage makes divorce seem to be a viable, attractive form of detachment. There are some counselors who recommend divorce as a way to ease the pain and escape from a seemingly incorrigible relationship, but this may not be the answer. A temporary separation may be in order to allow the partners to detach, to get good counseling, and to develop biblical convictions about marriage. Too often, a hurting codependent will dump one spouse only to find another to control and rescue, and the codependent cycle continues.

This is a sticky, emotion-charged issue. There are many views that are strongly held. The scope of this book doesn't include an adequate treatment of divorce, separation, and remarriage, but you may want to read *Jesus and Divorce*, by Bill Heth and Gordon Wenham, or *Love Must Be Tough*, by James Dobson. Before you make any major decisions about divorce, consult a competent, qualified Christian counselor or pastor.

How can you tell if you are detached?

It would be ludicrous to say that you haven't detached until you are perfectly calm and loving in your attitudes. With detachment often comes a range of emotions which, in the early stages, are often quite confusing. Nonetheless, you can tell that you are detaching if you have removed yourself from situations to feel and think, if there is a growing objectivity about the contrast between codependent reactions and healthy responses, and if you are experiencing a growing sense of independence.

When you can identify your codependent feelings and behaviors, and then think clearly and objectively about them, you are detaching. Recognize your guilt, fear, rescuing and controlling tendencies, and realize that these are the pathology of codependency. Don't dabble with them. Aggressively replace them with objectivity and godly choices. Then you will be detaching.

Become attached to the Lord

Detaching involves change: changing our perceptions, our values, our relationships, our view of ourselves, and our view of others. Being dependent upon the approval of others is changed to independence from others, but it also involves a growing dependence on the Lord.

183

As we detach from others, we can become attached to the Lord and deepen our relationship with Him because He is all we have longed for. He is loving and kind, strong and wise. He is not condemning, aloof, and manipulative. He can be trusted.

The affirmation and objectivity of a consistent friend

Detaching is difficult. It is almost impossible to do alone. As we discussed in chapter 12, you need a friend to help you be objective, to encourage you, and to model a healthy lifestyle. A true friend won't change the way he feels and acts toward you as you go through this difficult process. He will encourage you.

Develop habits of detaching

Don't be too discouraged if your first attempts at detaching are painful and awkward. Drastic change takes time, patience, practice, and courage. The more you try to detach, the more confident you will become, and eventually, it will become a very constructive habit for you.

My friend, Jim Walter, showed me some statements that describe both the process and the product of detachment. These statements are about "letting go":

"LET GO"

to "let go" does not mean to stop caring;
it means I can't do it for someone else

to "let go" is not to cut myself off;
it's the realization that I can't control another

to "let go" is not to enable,
but to allow learning from natural consequences

to "let go" is to admit powerlessness—which means the outcome
is not in my hands

to "let go" is not to try to change or blame another;
it's to make the most of myself

to "let go" is not to "care for," but to "care about"

to "let go" is not to judge, but to allow another to be a human being

to "let go" is to not be in the middle, arranging all the outcomes, but to allow others to affect their own destinies

to "let go" is not to be protective; it's to permit another to face reality

to "let go" is not to deny, but to accept

to "let go" is not to nag, scold or argue, but instead to search out my own shortcomings and correct them

to "let go" is not to adjust everything to my desires, but to take each day as it comes, and cherish myself in it

to "let go" is not to criticize and regulate anybody, but to try to become what I dream I can be

to "let go" is to not regret the past, but to grow and live for the future

to "let go" is to fear less and love more

Questions

1. What does it mean, *to detach*? Why is it important to detach?

2. What are some similarities and differences between withdrawing and detaching?

3. Describe some of your usual codependent responses in regard to the following:

   a) Feelings:

   b) Thoughts:

   c) Actions:

4. Make a list of questions that will help you feel and think clearly as you detach:

5. Make a list of statements that will remind you of your independence and identity:

6. Think of three recent situations in which you exhibited codependent reactions. How could you have detached in each situation? (Be specific: time, place, content.) What difference might it have made had you detached?

   a) Situation 1:

   b) Situation 2:

   c) Situation 3:

7. Which "Perspective on Detaching" stood out to you? Why?

Three Ingredients:

No. 3: Decide

It is possible to detach, to feel, to think and to consider your options, but then to be immobilized and not make any decision at all. After we have reflected, we need the courage to act in positive, healthy ways. We need to *stop* rescuing and controlling, and *start* saying and doing those things that reflect independence, security, strength, and health. This is extremely important, both for our own sake *and* for the sake of those we typically rescue and control.

In this chapter, we will examine a process that you can use to help you take steps toward emotional and relational health. The process has four components: making independent choices, setting limits, surrendering control of others, and enjoying life.

Making Independent Choices

Several months ago, I received a call from the booking agent of a music group we had contracted to perform at a conference. We had worked out the contract months earlier, and as a part of that contract, the group had agreed to obtain their own housing. Now, Sheila, the agent, explained, "We really tried to get housing for the group, but we just couldn't find any. You'll have to get it for us."

The more we talked, the more pity I felt for Sheila and the group. I could feel the pangs of guilt as I wrestled with saying no. Our budget was tight, and I knew we couldn't afford to pay for their housing. We wouldn't have agreed to the contract in the first place if we'd thought we'd have to shell out the money for that. But my desire to rescue and my sense of guilt won. Instead of saying no, I said, "I'll see what I can do," and hung up the phone.

I sat in my office and stewed. I wasn't angry with Sheila. I was angry with *myself*. I had done it again! I had rescued instead of being objective.

I took a few minutes to think about what had happened. I tried to sort out the facts objectively, and then I realized that we couldn't provide for the group's housing. We could take their housing costs out of their fee, or they could find their own housing. That was fair. It was objective. It was right. I called Sheila and told her that I had reconsidered the situation, and then explained my decision. I wasn't angry. I understood their predicament. But my decision was the right one. It wasn't my responsibility to take the time or spend the money to provide housing for the group.

Sheila was a little surprised that I called back so soon, but said she understood. In a week or so, she had worked out the details, and everything was just fine, thank you.

When we detach and become objective, we are able to admit how we feel. We can be angry, sad, glad, or afraid in a safe environment. And we are able to consider our options and make the best choice. Then we can act in confidence.

When we aren't sure of what to do, or when we feel pressured to react, we often use evasive language. A good friend of mine nailed me on this. Michael and I spent a lot of time together several years ago in Missouri. One day, another person asked me if I wanted to go to a party. I really didn't want to go, but to be polite (actually, to avoid offending the person and, therefore, avoid rejection) I said, "We'll see." Mike piped up and said, "When Pat says, 'We'll see,' he really means 'no'." Touche!

Making independent choices also means making honest statements, not using evasive language or double-talk. It is saying what we mean and meaning what we say.

Making independent choices also means that we can do helpful things for people because we *want* to, not just because we will feel guilty if we don't. A few weeks ago, my wife and I had our normally hectic morning getting the children ready for school and preparing for a staff meeting at home. Joyce came down the stairs with two heaping baskets of dirty clothes. As she weaved her way through the breakfast room and the kitchen on her way to the garage (a.k.a. laundry room), I stopped her. "Wait a minute," I said, "I'll get that for you." As I took the baskets, a friend who was early for our staff meeting asked me, "Pat, are you rescuing Joyce, or are you helping her because you want to?"

I stopped to think about it. Then I said, "No, I'm doing it because I want to. She could do it herself, and that would be okay. I don't think I would have felt guilty if I hadn't carried the baskets."

Ah, the freedom of making independent choices: doing right things for right reasons!

The crucial question

The key to making sound, independent decisions is asking and determining the answer to this crucial question: *Lord, what do You want me to do?* This question, however, is confusing for the codependent because in his mindset, he usually assumes that the Lord wants him to rescue and control others. He feels guilty if he doesn't do absolutely everything he possibly can for people—and often, he feels guilty even though he does.

Seeking the Lord's direction is still valid for codependents, but our mindset needs to change. That's what detaching is all about. Don't assume that the Lord always wants you to rescue, help, and/or control people. His primary concern is that we renounce idolatrous behavior in our relationships; that we stop trying to please others in an attempt to gain security and worth from *them* instead of from *Him*. When we are independent from the control of others, then we are open to the Lord's wisdom and direction. Then we can be objective about the question: *Lord, what do You want me to do?*

Codependents normally take responsibility for others but not for themselves. (The first time someone told me this, I thought he was crazy because I saw myself as a *very* responsible person. I didn't realize that I expected other people to make me happy while I felt responsible for making them happy.) With the Lord's direction and strength, we need to take responsibility for our *own* lives. If we have been passive, we need to take steps of action. If we have been driven, we need to learn to say no to some things, even if others don't understand or approve. If we have been saviors, we need to let others experience the consequences of their behavior. If we have felt like a Judas, we need to build our confidence by focusing on the unconditional love and acceptance of Christ. If we have acted like children, we need to start acting like adults.

Take steps to be responsible for your own life and honor the Lord in your personal life, relationships, goals, and habits. Develop a healthy independence from the bondage of pleasing others and a godly dependence on the love, wisdom, and strength of the Lord. This process begins when we ask the crucial question, *Lord what do You want me to do?*

Setting Limits

A vital part of healthy living is recognizing our limitations and setting realistic limits in our relationships with others. My friend, Mark Baker, has a very helpful analogy about the lack of limits in a codependent's life. He says that every person is given a piece of land when he is born, but a codependent allows people to take water from the property, cut down its trees, and trample its pasture. In fact, he encourages people to take advantage of his land, all in the hope of winning their approval. When his house has been burned, his crops and pastures trampled, and everything has been stolen, he finally gets angry and determines to set limits. At first, he doesn't let anyone even set foot on his property. He guards it with his rifle to be sure no one takes advantage of him again. After he has rebuilt his home, planted new crops, and become established again, he will be more willing to let people on his land. But even then, he will ensure that others do not take advantage of him.

Codependent behavior has very few limits. We feel responsible for everyone and everything. We try to help everybody. We feel guilty about everything. But as our sense of identity, independence, and objectivity grows, we will quickly realize that we can't continue life without limits. We need to set limits clearly and firmly, such as:

- This is what I will do. This is what I won't do.
- I will not take this kind of behavior anymore.
- I'm not responsible for his (her) happiness.
- I refuse to be manipulated.
- I'm sorry, I wish I could help you, but I can't.
- Why did you say that to me? Do you know how I feel when you say things like that?
- I don't want to talk about this.
- I want to talk about this.

Also, instead of anticipating the needs of others and jumping in to rescue them, you can listen patiently and wait for them to ask for your help. Then, you can make a decision about whether to help or not. Often, people explain their troubles and wait for you to volunteer to help without even being asked. (That's what you've done before!) Melanie Ahlquist advises people to be patient, not to rescue compulsively. If others want help, let them ask for it; then you can make an objective decision.

"But this seems so selfish!" someone might say about setting limits. "They need me! What about being a servant and going the extra mile?" Again, the question is: What is a rescuing, compulsive, codependent reaction to others' needs, and what is a healthy, independent, loving response? Inherent in this compulsive sense of being needed is the idea that *It's all up to me,* and *If I don't help him, who will?*

Can the Almighty, Omnipotent, Sovereign Lord take care of that person you are so determined to rescue? Are you so indispensable that you take the place of God? You may, indeed, be hindering that person's development of responsibility and independence by continually rescuing him. And you may also be blocking his, as well as your own dependence on God to provide and protect. It's not up to you! The Lord can take care of that person, and He can take care of you as you learn to identify, detach, and objectively decide to be independent of compulsive rescuing.

Stop Controlling Others

Just as you are seeking to make your own independent decisions, give other people the freedom to make their own choices. Don't try to control them. Too often we have tried to control the attitudes and behavior of others by praise and condemnation. And since most people live for acceptance, our manipulation has often worked. Now, as you are learning to be independent and make your own decisions, you can help others to do the same.

Calmly and clearly let people know what the consequences of their decisions will be. Love them, encourage them, but let them know that their choices make a difference. Instead of yelling or withdrawing, say something like, "That hurt me a lot. If you say things like that to me, it will hurt our relationship," or, "If you continue to treat me that way, I don't want to see you," or, "Until you have proven that you are responsible, I won't trust you to do this or that."

The pattern of controlling with praise and condemnation, anger and withdrawal, and overt expressions or subtle gestures is used extensively on children. It works most of the time, but the intensity is usually raised as the child tests his limits and gets used to each level of manipulation. Calm, loving discipline is much different from codependent manipulation, allowing the child to develop much needed responsibility and learn the consequences of his own behavior. Trying to control him through praise and condemnation may prevent his ability to see situations clearly and make objective decisions. And in adulthood, he will probably treat his children the same way. The cycle will then continue.

Some of the consequences of codependent living are difficult, both for us and for those in our families. Years of alcohol or drug addiction can result in the reality of financial collapse. Bitterness, manipulation, and lying often result in broken relationships and estrangement. The emotional trauma of guilt, hurt, anger, and loneliness are deep wounds that aren't easily mended. There are no quick and easy answers to these problems, but we can pick up the pieces, find a friend to help us, and trust the Lord to give us a fresh start.

Enjoying Life

Enjoying life is the fourth component in the process of developing emotional and relational health. As we grow in our independence and objectivity, we will begin to feel free and spontaneous. Instead of being driven to please others—and often being disappointed by their response—we will begin to experience unconditional love from God and from a new set of friends. We will begin to enjoy life; really enjoy life!

Many of the things that have seemed so desperately important will fade in their importance. Love, intimacy, spontaneity, and new goals and dreams will take their place. The perverted self-denial that characterized our lives will change to healthy giving and receiving. One man told me that anytime he was offered something, even ice cream, his first response was to refuse it. "Why?" I queried. "I don't know," he said. "I guess I just didn't think I was worthy of receiving a gift or having fun." Now, he's learning to value himself, to give freely, and to receive with freedom and gratitude. He's beginning to enjoy life.

What would you enjoy? What have you withheld from yourself because you deem yourself as unworthy? What goals and dreams can replace the driven and compulsive desires of codependency? What can you do this week (today!) just for the fun of it? Go out to dinner. Buy a game. Go to a movie. Buy a canoe. (I did!) Take a vacation. Tell a joke. Laugh. Help somebody because you *want* to. Dream new dreams. Make new friends. Relax. (This may sound like prosperity theology or blatant hedonism, but it's not. The encouragement for a guilt-ridden, overly responsible person to relax and have some fun is meant to give balance and health to his life, not hedonism.)

I heard a pastor tell a story recently that relates to this new, independent life we can have. He described his lawn in Southern California. In the summer, the oppressive heat bakes the grass, and it begins to turn brown. The months go by with very little rain, then the Santa Anna winds bring more heat in the late fall. By mid-winter, the yard looks barren. Not a green blade can be seen anywhere. The flowers have wilted long ago. The lawn is lifeless...or so it seems.

Then, in the spring, the rains begin. At first the lawn looks like a large mud puddle, but after a couple of weeks, a few sprigs of green begin to appear out of the muck. Then, almost overnight, the grass sprouts and spreads very quickly. There is life again!

Many of us are like that yard in mid-winter. We feel emotionally, spiritually, and relationally dry and barren. There hasn't been much sign of life for a good while, and we've just about given up hope. When the refreshment of encouragement and objectivity come our way, the grip of codependency doesn't give up easily. There doesn't seem to be much of a change for a while. Then a few sprigs of new life appear, and then a few more. If the rains continue, a full lawn will replace what was only barren ground a relatively short time before. There is hope, and life, and depth, and intimacy, and reality, and love!

As you identify your unusual codependent reactions, detach to feel and think clearly, and then decide to act courageously, you will begin to experience this kind of transformation. It may be slow at first, but with the encouragement of a friend, and the love and power of God, it will happen!

A Practical Exercise

A very practical exercise may be the impetus you need to follow through on your decisions. After you have completed the questions at the end of this chapter, write down several things to do on a 3x5 card. Make them very specific, and if possible, have one from each of the four components of the process in this chapter. For instance, you might write:

- Give my opinion (without vacillating) to my mother.
- If John asks me to lend him more money, I will say no.
- I am not going to tell Suzanne how to act. She needs to make her own choices.
- I'm going to ask Fred to tell me a joke today.
- I'm going out to lunch.

Keep this 3x5 card with you to remind you to act in a strong, independent, and healthy way. Change the statements on the card whenever you want to and after a while, you will develop a habit of making independent choices, setting limits, surrendering your control of others, and enjoying life more.

Questions

1. Name some differences between codependent and independent choices:

2. What does the Lord want you to do about your codependency? In your relationships?

3. Make a list of statements that will enable you to set and maintain limits. How will these help you?

4. List some benefits of stating consequences instead of controlling people:

5. In what ways do you enjoy life? In what ways do you not enjoy life?

6. How can you apply the three ingredients: *identify, detach,* and *decide,* today?

7. What statements can you put on a 3x5 card to help you take some practical steps to act in a strong, healthy way?

PART THREE

THE PROCESS

Sixteen

Emerging

Almost twenty years ago, Elisabeth Kübler-Ross wrote a book about the process that terminal cancer patients experience as they come to terms with their disease. The process of coping with the physical disease closely parallels that of dealing with emotional difficulties. The authors of several books have used this process to describe how a person comes to grips with emotional trauma. Kübler-Ross does not come from an orthodox Christian perspective (and her most recent book has a New Age slant), but her insights into the grief process are very insightful nonetheless. We will apply this process, or a variation of it, to a person's emergence from the blackness of codependency.

Effectively dealing with traumatic, emotional difficulties includes five stages: denial, bargaining, anger, grief, and acceptance.[1] This is not a push-button, 1-2-3 kind of process. A person may move quickly through one phase, but very slowly through another. And he may go back and forth from time to time, re-entering a stage he has already gone through as he becomes aware of other pains and hurts he has not previously seen. Generally speaking, however, a person will not progress to the next stage until he has more or less fully experienced that which he is in. The following diagram may be helpful. Objectivity is the door which opens into the process. Acceptance is the door leading out of it and into health. In the middle are three vats, or containers, representing bargaining, anger, and grief. A person will not progress to constructive anger until he is through with bargaining, and he will not experience grief until he has spent his anger. (This, of course, does not mean that the person does not experience anger or grief except in that phase. It only means that these emotions will be dominant during that time.)

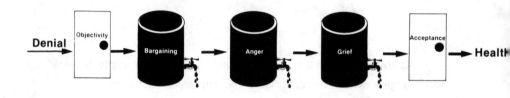

Let's examine each of these phases.

Denial

We devoted a good deal of space to this issue in chapter 3, so we won't rehash each point here, but we will briefly recap some of the reasons why codependents live without objectivity.

• We don't have a viable point of comparison to contrast pathological codependent behavior with healthy behavior. We think our families, our circumstances, our thoughts, our emotions, and our behavior are "normal."

• We may have developed an unconscious defense mechanism of staying so busy that we don't have time to reflect and feel pain. Many of us are driven people; driven to accomplish our own goals, and those established by organizations, corporations, and others. This compulsion is a vain attempt to block pain and gain a sense of self-worth.

• Some us us have become passive and emotionally numb in our effort to block pain. We avoid decisions and relationships when the risk of failure and rejection seems too high. (Actually, most of us use some combination of compulsion and passivity in our attempts to cope with codependency.)

• Some of us are so crushed, so hopeless, so depressed, that we don't believe anything good can or will ever happen to us. We withdraw into a cocoon of morbid introspection and self-hatred.

• Some have been sheltered, protected from the pains and joys of life. One man said: "My parents didn't let me make any decisions. They always decided what I would do, where I would go, which classes I would take, which hobbies and sports I would be involved in...everything! They would say things like, 'We're not going to let you go out for football because you wouldn't be very good at it. You'd fail, then you'd be disappointed, and we'd be disappointed, too.' For me, failure was pre-determined because I had absolutely no confidence in myself. I am shy, insecure, and afraid to try anything because I might fail and let people down. To me, the worst thing that can happen is my disappointing someone by failing."

• The pain of neglect or condemnation is so great for some people that they recoil at being loved by someone. "Affirmation hurts. Love is painful. I can't take it!" said one sad woman.

• Some of us have so much repressed hurt and anger that we lose our tempers fairly often. These explosions are unlike the productive expressions that we will examine later in this chapter. They are not the product of understanding and objectivity. This anger is just the "tip of the iceberg," and is coupled with guilt and self-hatred, not healing forgiveness and understanding. Some people may say, "I must be pretty far along in the process. I'm really in touch with my anger," but in reality, they haven't even started the process because they have yet to see the root cause of their anger.

Objectivity is the door which enables us to enter the process of healing. Understanding the pathology of codependency and seeing its cumulative effects in our lives can be shocking at first, but that realization is necessary to participate in the rest of the process.

Bargaining

When a person gets a glimpse of the effects of codependency in his life, he will often respond by trying to bargain with himself, his family, and God. Christy learned about dysfunctional families from a close friend, and quickly saw those painful effects in her own life. At the end of the conversation, she was desperate for an answer. She blurted out, "Then how can I get my father to love me?" Her friend explained, "That's the wrong question, Christy. It's not up to you to get your father to love you. He is responsible for that. It's up to you to be independent and secure in the Lord, whether your father ever loves you or not."

Bargaining takes many shapes and forms, but its goal is to get other people to change by offering some change in ourselves. *I'll be a better husband to her. I'll spend more time with him. I won't nag him anymore, then he'll love me the way I want to be loved. I'll keep the house clean. I'll get a job. I'll be more affectionate.* We can come up with all kinds of "deals" to get people to love us, but bargaining is still not totally objective. The responsibility still remains on us alone, and we are still believing the best about the other person.

Believing the best of others is usually good and right. It is usually a virtue. But when a person has proven by months and years of irresponsible, manipulative behavior that he is pathological, then believing the best is not a virtue. It is naive and foolish. It is the haven of denial.

Bargaining is an expression of hope; hope that the other person will change and give us the love and worth that we need. But it is a false hope. The hard truth, the reality of objective observation, leads us to a painful but honest conclusion: we need to give up. We need to abandon the vain hope that the other person will change and give us what we need. Giving up doesn't sound very spiritual. It doesn't sound very godly, but it is. Giving up is a reflection of reality, and it is an act of abandoning the idol of pleasing others and being accepted and loved by them as the way to win self-worth. Actually, it is an act of worship to the Lord.

When we give up, when we stop bargaining and look the truth in the face, we may become very angry with the one who has lied to us, used us, and hurt us so deeply.

Anger

Anger is a difficult issue to write about. It is, by its nature, volatile and consuming. Many people hold strong but often contrasting opinions about it. Treatments of anger are sometimes superficial, and sometimes complex and confusing. Here's my best shot:

All anger is not wrong, nor is all anger right. Some of it is good and wholesome, but much of it is sin. There is a difference between feeling angry and acting angry. It isn't wrong to feel angry when it is a natural response to some type of pain in our environment. Some people see this anger as sin, and they either deny that it exists or they express it indirectly (passive aggression) and inappropriately. The active expression of anger can be either righteous or unrighteous. It can either hurt or heal. If the feeling of anger prompts us to stop being manipulated, to be independent of others, and to state our case clearly and calmly instead of withdrawing or attaching, then the response to that feeling is good and healthy. If, however, that feeling of anger prompts revenge and/or withdrawal, then the response is destructive. Two classic passages about anger are Eph. 4:26-27 and James 1:19-20.

Paul admonishes us to feel angry, but not to express that anger unrighteously:

> *BE ANGRY, AND yet DO NOT SIN; do not let the sun go down on your anger, and do not give the devil an opportunity."*   Eph. 4:26-27

James warns us not to let our expression of anger hurt others:

> *This you know, my beloved brethren. But let everyone be quick to hear, slow to speak and slow to anger; for the anger of man does not achieve the righteousness of God.*
>   James 1:19-20

For our purposes, we will differentiate between destructive anger and constructive anger. *Destructive anger* is based on the desire to harm another person. It consists of outbursts, rage, seething, and revenge. *Constructive anger* is the result of being harmed by another. Too often, however, we cross over the line in our response, and constructive anger quickly becomes destructive. That's why Paul wrote, *Be angry* (constructive anger), *and yet do not sin* (destructive anger).

Most of us have mixed perceptions about anger. If we have repressed it for a long time, it may surface in embarrassing ways. So we rationalize it. We feel guilty about it. We ignore it. We hate ourselves for it. In general, most of us have consciously or unconsciously come to the conclusion that anger is wrong. In this process of our healing, we may try to skip from anger to grief because grief seems more acceptable. But we won't be able to thoroughly grieve until we have come to grips with the reality of our anger.

Codependents have difficulty with anger because present offenses are complicated and compounded by a backlog of repressed anger at past offenses. The command: *Do not let the sun go down on your anger* has been violated so many times that denial and repression have become the normal way of dealing with anger. The answer is objectivity and honesty about that repressed anger, but we cannot dredge up every offense of the past and deal with them in a day. It takes longer than that! After a period of honest reflection and honest expression of repressed emotions, we are then able to deal effectively with each offense as it occurs, not letting "the sun go down" on our anger.

Perhaps a diagram will help describe how repressed anger makes it difficult to deal effectively with present offenses.

The response to a new offense is complicated and compounded by a backlog of past offenses. Most of us either repress our anger at the new offense, too, or respond in anger that is disproportionate to the offense.

Through being honest about repressed anger and expressing it in a safe environment, the backlog is gradually diminished.

Eventually, our backlog of anger is expressed and dealt with. Because new offenses are not complicated by repressed anger, we can respond more objectively with appropriate anger and forgiveness (Eph. 4:26-27).

In the unconditional love and acceptance of God, we have an environment in which we can be honest and vulnerable. We not only can acknowledge our present hurt and anger, but we can be objective about the cumulative hurts of the past—and the resulting anger that has been stored inside us. David instructs us to be open and honest with God because He cares for us:

> *Trust in Him at all times, O people; pour out your heart before*
> *Him; God is a refuge for us.*   Ps. 62:8

Many codependents stop their progress at this phase of the process because they have developed an aversion to expressing anger—especially about the one who has offended them the most. Unless this impasse can be broken, they will not proceed to grief, acceptance, and ultimately to stability and health. Here are a few reasons people can't or won't be angry:

- They believe: *All anger is wrong and sinful. If I am angry, then I must be a bad person.*
- They believe: *If there is any problem in the relationship, it must be my fault!* They feel a misguided, blind loyalty to the one who has deeply hurt them. This loyalty is coupled with pangs of guilt at even the thought of being angry with him or her.
- They excuse the offense: *Oh, that's okay. I don't mind. It doesn't hurt me. I'm used to it by now, and besides, she couldn't help it.*
- They are afraid of the backlash of anger, rejection, ridicule, withdrawal, and wrath of the other person.
- They are afraid that after experiencing healing, warmth, and intimacy in the relationship, they will be hurt all over again; too great a risk.
- Being angry is not an option that they will even consider. Often, seething anger and bitter hurt are repressed. In their denial, codependents won't acknowledge any problem at all.
- In their lack of objectivity, they only see the good things about the other person. They either don't see anything harmful, selfish, or negative, or if they do, they quickly rationalize those characteristics.
- They have been taught by some Bible teachers that their par-

ents or spouse is their authority, and that they must unconditionally submit to them. In a dysfunctional family, this submission is used to manipulate, condemn, and use the codependent.

It is very important to find a safe environment of unconditional love and acceptance to develop honesty about the cumulative effects of repressed anger in your life. Constructive anger occasionally moves to destructive anger. You need someone to give you both affirmation and correction. Exposing hurts and anger can be awkward and difficult, and will take time. However, at the heart of this constructive anger and pain is a sense of stability that is based on objectivity. Even though it can be tremendously painful to express these emotions, you are still likely to experience a sense of satisfaction in knowing why you've struggled so much for so long. After your anger is spent, however, you will likely feel a sense of loss.

Grief

"There is a little girl in me who was never loved by her father," Susan said sadly, "and she never will be."

Will said, "I had such hopes and dreams for our marriage, but now it will never be what I hoped it would be. I feel so empty."

"Our darling little girl was so cute, so loving," Margaret said, as she remembered her daughter. "But drugs have ruined her life...and almost ruined ours, too. We'll just have to make the best of it now."

When the vat of anger has been drained to a trickle, a sense of loss begins to dominate us. We grieve as if someone had died because it seems like someone did...us. We had something and it was taken away. Or we realize that we have wanted something—love and acceptance from a certain person—very badly, but will never have it. We wanted intimacy, warmth, and laughter, but we feel only hurt and emptiness.

Janice was progressing through this process, and she described her grief to me: "I was sitting in church one day and I had the strangest feeling. I felt like I was going to cry and throw up at the same time. I thought, *I'm losing it! I'm really going crazy!* After the service, I realized that I was grieving. I guess that I've bottled up my emotions for so long that they came out in a strange way."

Over the next several months, Janice continued to grieve. She felt sad. She felt lonely. But she also knew that this was a part of the process. She really wasn't going crazy. She was becoming healthy!

How do we grieve? How long do we grieve? Good questions, but there are no clear and simple answers. There are no formulas for grieving. We grieve by giving ourselves the freedom to feel loss for as long as it takes. It helps greatly to have someone to affirm you and give you perspective (Does this sound like a broken record?) as you go through this process. You need someone who will listen to you and comfort you without giving quick and easy solutions to get you to feel better.

Months may go by. Your emotions will vary. Sometimes you will feel the catharsis of the healing process, but sometimes, you will feel very sad. You may become emotional over things that never affected you before—an act of kindness toward you, a crying child, a new offense. All of this is normal and healthy. It is part of being a real person with real feelings in real relationships. The Lord will give you grace and comfort. Then you will be able to accept all that has happened to you.

Acceptance

Finally, we experience a sense of peace and calm. The bargaining, anger, and grief have been exposed and expressed. We are objective about life: its good and bad, its righteousness and wickedness. We are uncomfortable with simple, easy answers knowing that they just don't work.

We gain a new depth in our relationship with the Lord and with people. We discover new perspectives on life, new values, and new lifestyles. We don't feel driven to accomplish every goal because we have a new set of priorities. We enjoy a healthy blend of independence from others and a new dependence on the Lord. We can say no, and we can admit being wrong.

People who can see their lives with objectivity can help others be objective, too. There is wisdom in their perceptions, and they can comfort those who hurt because they understand their hurts (2 Cor. 1:3-5).

Mark asked, "When I get to that phase, will I experience total freedom? Will I be completely free from the effects of my codependency, or will I always be scarred?" I thought for a minute, then I told Mark about an incident in my life years ago.

When I was young, our family bought some Roman candles to shoot on New Year's Eve. My father lit them and off they flew into the night, exploding in all kinds of colors. I had been parked under the arm of my mother on the front steps, but lighting the fireworks looked like lots of fun, so after my father lit one, I ran down the steps and grabbed it. I held it straight up, waiting for it to blast up into the sky. Instead, it backfired inside the sleeve of the winter jacket I was wearing!

Like it was yesterday, I vividly remember looking through sheets of tears at my parents. They grabbed me and took me inside to see how badly I was hurt. It was worse than they could have imagined. At the hospital, they learned that I had third-degree burns over most of my forearm.

For the next several months, the burn required almost constant attention. Wrapping, unwrapping, putting on medicine, making trips to the doctor, crying in the night. My exuberant little sprint to grab the firework had resulted in agony for the whole family. After a few months, scar tissue began to form on the burn. Gradually, the burn required less and less attention.

Today, there is still a sizable scar on my arm, but I rarely think about it until I see someone staring at it in the summer when I'm wearing a short-sleeved shirt. Though the scar remains, the pain has been gone for years, and the consuming attention it required is just a memory.

Codependency is a deep wound that requires a lot of attention for a while. Even the emotional bandaging and medication seem to hurt, but if it is well-treated, scar tissue will gradually form as the healing process continues. Though the scar may remain, the pain will gradually be replaced by healing and health. This process isn't pleasant, but it is essential if the wound is to heal.

Questions

1. Why do we try to bargain to get people to love us?

2. Why is bargaining a false hope? Why is it important to give up?

3. Describe the differences between destructive and constructive anger:

4. What are some ways a person can deal with a backlog of repressed anger?

5. Look at the reasons why many of us won't or can't be honest about our anger. Do any of these apply to you? If so, which one(s)? How will understanding this roadblock help you?

6. What might grief be like and feel like for you?

7. What are some changes that might happen in your life when you get to the acceptance phase?

8. Which phase are you in now? How can you tell?

9. What (or whom) do you need to help you through this process?

Seventeen

Relating to the "Other Person": Lordship or Love

One of the most pressing issues for the person who is emerging from the darkness of codependency is: *How do I relate to the one who has hurt, neglected, used, and condemned me?* Relating to "that other person" (a parent, spouse or any significant other) is where "the rubber meets the road" in our growth and freedom. Our growing objectivity and honest emotions produce a cataclysmic upheaval in our lives. Relating to that particular person is often the most difficult part of the whole process.

Most of the issues we will examine in this chapter have been expressed in other chapters, but at the risk of being redundant, I think it is wise to draw some of these thoughts together here. The primary issue is idolatry or independence: are we going to continue to let a person determine our behavior and thus, be our lord, or are we going to be independent and make our own decisions, including loving him or her unconditionally?

Idolatry or Independence

Most of us have erroneously defined love in the context of codependency. We have thought of love as rescuing, worrying, feeling guilty, being compliant to manipulation, and pitying that other person whom we care for. The desire to be accepted and the desire for intimacy have been so strong that we would do anything to make that person happy. We've called it love. It's not. It's idolatry. It's bondage. We have allowed a person to be our lord and to determine our thoughts, feelings, words, and actions.

Comments from people who are finally being objective about this bondage reveal the depth of this lordship:

One woman lamented: "I've lived to please my father all of my life. He said, 'Jump!' and I said, 'How high?' No, I didn't even ask, 'How high?' I just jumped as high as I could as often as I could. I got some praise for what I did, just enough to keep me jumping, but not enough to give me a sense of security."

Terry remembered: "My mother always could get me to do anything she wanted me to do. She rarely yelled at me, but she could get a powerful message across with the expressions on her face."

Brad talked about his daughter: "I did everything I could do to get her to stop eating. I begged, I threatened, I hid food, I sent her to classes, I screamed at her, I avoided her. I can't tell you how many nights I lay awake trying to think of ways to get her to stop. I thought she was the one who was 'hooked,' but I was an addict, too; an addict to her performance and happiness."

Dan hadn't gotten to the part of objectivity yet. He looked puzzled at the thought of independence and the idea of letting his wife live with the consequences of her actions. "She needs me. What would happen to her if I didn't help her?"

There is only One who is worthy of our ultimate affection and obedience. If we put others in His place, if we try to please others as a means of gaining love and value, then we are committing idolatry. Paul wrote to the believers in Corinth that pleasing Christ is worthy of our ambitions:

> *Therefore also we have as our ambition, whether at home or absent, to be pleasing to Him.* 2 Cor. 5:9

Paul also wrote to the Galatians to remind them of the difference between pleasing people and pleasing Christ:

> *For am I now seeking the favor of men, or of God? Or am I*
> *striving to please men? If I were still trying to please men, I*
> *would not be a bond-servant of Christ.*
>
> Gal. 1:10

Once we have trusted Christ, and accepted His payment for our sins, our identity is secure in Him. We are His beloved children, recipients of His unconditional love, forgiveness, and acceptance. As we experience His grace, we will become willing bondservants and enjoy a healthy independence from the bondage of pleasing others.

It may be difficult or painful, but we need to be objective about our relationship with that "other person." Call a spade a spade. Call it idolatry. Don't try to bargain. Don't try to get that person to give you the love and acceptance he or she has never given even though you have tried so hard to get it. Turn from that idolatry by getting your significance and worth from Christ alone. Then, and only then, will you be able to respond to that person the way the Lord wants you to, in objectivity, healthy independence, forgiveness, and unconditional love.

Responding in a Healthy,
Realistic Way

Your relationship with that particular person you care for has probably been characterized by some combination of rescuing, outbursts of anger, displaced anger, compliance, withdrawal, guilt, hurt, loneliness, pity for him, and pity for yourself. A sense of loyalty has probably contributed to your inability to see the relationship objectively. You may have thought that any negative thoughts or emotions (even though you've had many of them) are signs that there is something dreadfully wrong—with you!

Now you are growing in your objectivity. You are learning that you've repressed emotions that you didn't even know existed. This is difficult, but you're getting in touch with your feelings. Your source of security is changing. You're learning to make your own decisions. All of these are good things, but there's *that* person: your spouse, your sibling, your parent, your child, your classmate, who has hurt you deeply. What do you do? What do you say?

Remember to identify, detach, and decide. Recognize how you feel and how you act when you see or think of that person. Then detach so you have the time and space necessary to think and feel. You may be able to detach calmly, but you may not. Even if you have to detach in anger, remember that not detaching is prolonging idolatry. So, detach. Ask yourself questions so you will see what is really going on. Then make your own choices about what to say and do.

Set limits. Decide what you can live with for right now. Decide on the extent of your communication and contact with that person. Determine which issues you will discuss and which ones you won't. If you decide on these ahead of time, you will be much less likely to succumb to the pressure of the moment and give in to manipulation or condemnation. The relationship has been on his or her terms for perhaps your whole life, but it can be on your terms now. (This isn't selfish. Remember, *you're* the one who is trying to live in reality, not the other person. It is perfectly good and right to insist on making your own decisions based on reality. Too often, we have believed lies, lived by deception, and made our codependent decisions to rescue and feel guilty based on a world of unreality. This can now end. Base your life on what is *really* real, not on what a dysfunctional person believes and says is real.)

How much do you say? Do you tell that person all about codependency and how messed up you've been because of your relationship with him? Do you describe your dark thoughts, your bitterness, hatred, and fear? The principle here is: express yourself fully to God, and express yourself appropriately to the other person. As you recall, David encouraged us to: *Trust in Him at all times...Pour out your heart before Him...* (Ps. 62:8), but we are *not* to pour out our hearts to *people*. Only a fool delights in telling everything he knows: *A fool does not delight in understanding, but only in revealing his own mind* (Prov. 18:2). The question is not: *How much can I blast him?* but rather, *What will help that person? How much does he need to know at this time and this place?*

You may tell that person a lot or very little. As your response to him changes, he may ask you what's going on. But he may not. As you consider what to do in this relationship, seek the advice of a mature, godly, knowledgeable person to give you perception and encouragement.

Don't expect to do all of this perfectly (you perfectionist, you!). Give yourself a break! *All* of this is new. Because this is such a contrast to how you have related in the past, you can expect to have all kinds of conflicting thoughts and emotions.

And don't expect the other person to say, "Well, now I completely understand. Thank you so much for saying all of this. I'll change today and never treat you the same way again." He may say he'll change, but that's what he's said a hundred times before. He may weep and try to elicit your pity. He may withdraw from you. He may say, "Let's talk about this," but he probably doesn't really want to understand your point of view. He probably wants to convince you that you are wrong (poor, misguided, confused person that you are) so that you will return to being the docile, compliant puppet you've always been.

Or he may say, "It's all your fault." The denial of personal responsibility is a common characteristic in manipulative, condemning people. Scott Peck described such people in his book, *People of the Lie*. He wrote that they do not recognize their "dark side," that propensity to evil that all of us have. They are so steeped in denial that they cannot even see how they manipulate and condemn others. They may say, "I'm sorry," but what they mean is, *I'm sorry you feel that way. I've never done anything wrong, but you have!* They want quick, superficial forgiveness so the relationship can go back to its pathological status quo.

When we detach from that "other person," it is usually awkward. Karen said, "I can't even pray for him anymore. I feel so strange. I know what I'm doing is right, but shouldn't I be able to pray for him?" She was feeling guilty and confused. Her friend helped her to understand the situation more clearly. "That's okay, Karen. God can take care of him without your prayers. He wants you to concentrate on detaching and getting your security from Him for now. Later, you can start praying for him again." Your life is changing, so expect a variety of changes in your thoughts and emotions. It's all a part of the process.

Realistic expectations are vital to your relationship. He or she may change, but it is foolish to expect resolution and reconciliation very soon, if ever. Let your identity in Christ and His lordship fill your thoughts, not dreams of intimacy with "that person." He or she may never change, but you can. You can be unhooked. You can be independent, healthy, and realistic.

Excusing or Forgiving

As codependents, we have been quick to excuse people for how they have hurt us. Excusing, though, is not forgiving. Forgiveness acknowledges the reality of the offense, the full weight of the wrong, and the consequences of the wrong. It then chooses to not hold that offense against the person. When Christ died on the cross, His blood was the payment for our sins so we could be truly forgiven, not just excused for our sins. Our forgiveness of others can mirror the depth of that forgiveness. Paul wrote:

> *Let all bitterness and wrath and anger and clamor and slander be put away from you, along with all malice. And be kind to one another, tender-hearted, forgiving each other, just as God in Christ also has forgiven you.*
>
> Eph. 4:31-32

Forgiveness does not imply that you have to trust the one you have forgiven. Some of us link the two. We believe, *If I can't trust him, then I haven't really forgiven him.* That belief, however, is not true, and it causes undue pressure and guilt. If a person has proven over the course of months or years that he is untrustworthy, then he can be forgiven, but he should not be trusted. Trusting a proven liar is foolishness, not godliness.

Similarly, understanding is not the same as forgiving. Understanding the painful background of those who have hurt us is often a helpful perception, but most codependents respond in pity, excusing harmful behavior and feeling guilty for being angry. In that case, we have understood, but we haven't forgiven.

Beth had been married to Timothy for four years. Timothy was a compulsive workaholic who spent eighty hours a week at the office, and thought about work-related problems when he was at home. Beth had put up with it for a long time, even encouraging him because he was doing so well in his position. But after four years, enough was enough. At the time that Beth was becoming exasperated with Timothy's work habits and neglect of his family, the couple visited his parents at Christmas. On previous visits, Beth had noticed how Timothy's father seemed to be busy most of the time with projects around the house. He had built them a dresser when they were married and several other things as the years had gone by.

Beth now looked at her father-in-law with a more jaundiced eye. *He is a workaholic, too. That's why Timothy is the way he is! No wonder he works so hard. That's all he has ever seen in his father. And Timothy's father neglects his wife the same way Timothy neglects me.* That flash of insight helped put a lot of pieces together for Beth. She felt better. She understood.

As the months went by after their visit with Timothy's parents, Beth tried to excuse Timothy's neglect and preoccupation with his work. Soon, however, she realized that excusing him wasn't the same as forgiving him. She had begun to pity Timothy instead of loving him, but his behavior was wrong. It hurt. Instead of continuing to pity and excuse him, Beth forgave Timothy and committed herself to loving him unconditionally. That meant loving him enough to confront him with the reality of his workaholism and its effects on both of them.

Timothy didn't respond very well. He was angry and defensive, but he agreed to read a book and talk to their pastor about their relationship. After a while, Timothy began to recognize his addiction to success and performance. Together, he and Beth began to experience healing and intimacy in their relationship. It started with reality, forgiveness, unconditional love, and courage.

When a person first learns about codependency, there is a tendency for his view of the one who hurt him and manipulated him to flip-flop from white (he can do no wrong) to black (he can do no right). The anger generated by the realization of hurts, offenses, and damage is a motivation to detach, to stop the idolatry of the relationship, and to begin to establish a new, secure identity. As time goes by, however, greater objectivity will color in shades of gray where black has been before, and the codependent will be able to see the person who has hurt him more clearly. Anger will turn to grief, and grief, to acceptance and health. Then he will be able to see both the good and the bad in that person. He may continue to be manipulated and condemned. His relationship may still be void of trust and intimacy, but he will have confidence that he is living in reality with no grudges. No, it's not a fairy tale ending, but it is good and right and acceptable.

Questions

1. In what ways is a codependent's relationship with the "other person" idolatrous?

2. How would you have defined or described *love* in the past? How about now?

3. Describe your relationship with the person(s) who has hurt you deeply. How has he (she) treated you? How have you responded (emotions, thoughts, actions)?

4. What limits do you need to set in your relationship with that person?

5. Is it selfish to have the relationship on your terms now? Why, or why not?

6. How much should you say to him or her? How and when will you say it? How can you be well-prepared?

7. Describe the difference between excusing and forgiving that person:

8. What do you need to know, be, or do to respond to him or her in a healthy, independent, loving, realistic way?

9. How do you realistically expect this person to respond?

* For additional insight, review chapters 13, 14, and 15: "Identify," "Detach," and "Decide."

Eighteen

The Reality of God

About two years ago, I was asked to go to India and Thailand to observe the Campus Crusade for Christ (CCC) ministry in those countries. For a week in New Delhi and Bangalore, India, we met godly men and women who are seeing thousands of Hindus, Jains, and Sikhs come to Christ. It was exciting to hear their stories! On the flight from Bangalore to Bangkok, I sat with Boonma Panthasri, the diminutive CCC director for Thailand. I was curious about his ministry in that predominantly Buddhist country.

I asked, "Boonma, how do you share Christ with Buddhists? How do you make the Gospel clear to them?"

Boonma replied, "Well, Pat, we show them that our God is bigger than their god."

"How do you do that?"

Without blinking an eye, Boonma replied, "We cast out their demons and heal their sick."

Being the conservative I am, I was a bit startled. "You do that?" I asked.

"Oh yes, all the time," he replied calmly.

At that point, I looked at the two Tylenol in my hand that I had just gotten for my headache. I looked at Boonma. I looked at the Tylenol again. And then with a muffled laugh, I decided not to ask him to heal my headache. I downed the Tylenol with a glass of water.

In the 150 years or so of Christendom in Thailand, 800 churches were started by 1980. In the decade since then, that number has more than doubled. The Lord is doing phenomenal things in that country through godly men and women like Boonma. These believers have a deep sense of intimacy with God and a strong dependence on Him. They are demonstrating profound humility, and yet a bold belief in God. These people have a strong sense of His presence and power.

I have far greater resources than Boonma in terms of technology, literature, and Christian presence in my culture, yet I often find myself feeling driven, pushed, and tired.

Many of us are self-sufficient people. We feel responsible for everybody and everything up to and including the INF treaty, but we feel guilty, alone, and fearful that we can't measure up. If we stop and look at our driven lives, we might wonder, *Where is God in all this? Why do I get so busy, frazzled, and burned-out? Do I really believe that I need God, or do I think I can do all of this by myself?* We look at Jesus' words to His disciples in Matt. 11:28-30:

> *Come to Me, all who are weary and heavy-laden, and I will give you rest. Take My yoke upon you, and learn from Me, for I am gentle and humble in heart; and you shall find rest for your souls. For My yoke is easy, and My load is light.*

...and we wonder, *Why isn't that true of me?*

In these pages, we have examined the cognitive and relational issues of codependency. Now we turn to the mystical issue: the reality of God.

Oh, we might all say that we believe in God, but at the same time, we may live as if He has checked out of the country. We feel alone and distant from Him.

In stark contrast, however, others go to the opposite extreme.

Instead of distance between themselves and God, they have become passive, expecting God to do everything for them.

Between these extremes is a proper biblical balance of our responsibility and God's empowerment; our part and God's part. But how did we lose our proper perspective of God in the first place?

Rationalism/Mysticism

The word *mysticism* is not being used here to refer to the extremes of emotionalism and passivity that characterize some groups of Christian believers. We are using the term to mean the experience of the presence and power of God, a sense of intimacy with Him and dependence on Him. This experience is not based on feelings, but is an awareness of His character and His power based on His Word.

Dr. Paul Hiebert, a professor at the Fuller Seminary School of World Missions, has observed that the Scriptures were written to a culture much like the Third World today, a culture that assumed the presence of the supernatural and its influence in the material world.[1] It is a three-tiered view of life: one, supernatural; one, material; and one that represents the interaction between the supernatural and the material world.

Western culture, in contrast, is based on a two-tiered approach: an upper tier of religion, a lower tier of empirical science, but an "excluded middle." There is little perception of God's direct and active involvement in the affairs of life. Increasingly, rationalism is king, and religion is compartmentalized and robbed of significance. The prevailing belief is, *If it can't be seen, felt, tasted, and observed, then it can't be real.* These diagrams are adapted from Dr. Hiebert's article. They illustrate the differences between the world view of the Third World and the Bible (on the left), and the world view of Western culture (on the right).

Supernatural (God, Satan, angels, demons, heaven, hell)	**Religion** (Supernatural, hypermystical)
Interaction between the supernatural and the material (Faith; seeing the reality of God in the physical world)	(Excluded middle)
Empirical (See, feel, taste, hear, smell)	**Science** (Empirical, material, natural)

A number of factors influence our view of life in the West. Humanism erodes our theological and philosophical base. Advanced technology leads us to believe that man can do anything; therefore, he doesn't need God. Materialism makes us think that success and possessions will ultimately satisfy us. And prosperity theology communicates that life should be easy and fun, leading to shallow, self-seeking believers who buy into the culture instead of standing out as light and salt in it.

Christians in our culture, and especially codependent Christians, tend to live by the two-tiered segmentation between materialistic naturalism and hypermysticism. We are either self-sufficient rationalists or hypermystical irrationalists. A balanced, biblical faith is elusive. This continuum shows the extremes, as well as biblical faith.

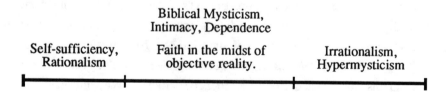

Biblical Mysticism,
Intimacy, Dependence

Self-sufficiency,
Rationalism

Faith in the midst of
objective reality.

Irrationalism,
Hypermysticism

The self-sufficient rationalist is a practical atheist, giving lip service to the reality of God but living as if there is no God. He finds his own solutions to the problems of life. He may be highly organized and driven to succeed, but he knows little of true intimacy and satisfaction. He focuses on the commands of the Scriptures.

The irrational, hypermystic tends to feel close to God, but often demonstrates an overdependence on feelings, impressions, and signs from God. Instead of being overly responsible, this person may be passive, waiting for God to give him everything he needs. He focuses on the promises of the Scriptures.

Sometimes, the codependent may feel very close to the Lord because he senses the unconditional love that he has never felt before. He also may be very easily disappointed if he feels like the Lord has let him down. This flip-flop from white to black in his relationship with God may happen regularly, or it may be so devastating that it takes years for him to recover.

Bruce is from a divorced family. He was driven to succeed, but even as he did, he still felt guilty and lonely. When he became a Christian, Bruce suddenly felt loved. He still carried the load of his codependent behavior, but for the first time in his life, he felt loved! He also felt very close to God.

Several months passed, and another crisis developed in Bruce's family. His mother's neglect and condemnation was driving a wedge in the family, and now much of it was directed at him because he was "so stupid to believe in that Christian stuff. Have you lost your mind? No, you never had one. This proves it!"

Bruce prayed long and hard, asking God to bring peace and love to his family. "You can do anything," Bruce prayed. "You can cause my mother to become a Christian and then our family can know Your love." At one point, Bruce felt that God had given him a promise from the Scriptures about his mother's salvation. He was jubilant! He told his Christian friends. They were happy for him, but seemed a bit cautious. Months went by, but his mother's intransigence was just as strong, and her attacks, just as bitter.

Bruce's exuberance turned to hope, then hope turned to pleading, and finally, his pleading turned to despair. There was no change. God had not worked. Bruce concluded that God wasn't trustworthy, after all. The closeness that he had felt with God evaporated, and he became depressed. The one bright spot in his life had turned to darkness.

Years later, Bruce learned about codependency and the grace of God. Slowly, he began to understand what had happened when "God had let him down." Bruce had wanted his mother to become a Christian so that she wouldn't keep condemning him. He had assumed that God would do whatever he wanted. It was a good, but immature perspective. The more he learned, the more his view of God and of himself changed, and mature biblical faith began to emerge.

Obviously, there are strengths and weaknesses in both extremes of rationalism and hypermysticism, but the biblical blend combines the desire and discipline of the rationalist with the intimacy and faith of the hypermystic. In the middle of the continuum is a balance of God's part and our part.

God's Part/Our Part

The apostle Paul had a clear grasp of the blend of our responsibility and God's empowerment. He realized that our best efforts cannot accomplish the work of the kingdom of God, yet we play an integral part in God's purposes on earth. Two passages come to mind immediately:

> *So then, my beloved, just as you have always obeyed, not as in my presence only, but now much more in my absence, work out your salvation with fear and trembling; for it is God who is at work in you, both to will and to work for His good pleasure.* Phil. 2:12-13

We are to work out (not work for) our salvation in fear and trembling. We have a responsibility to be faithful and obedient, but that responsibility is limited. God must work in and through us to accomplish what is of eternal value.

The second passage is Col. 1:29:

And for this purpose also I labor, striving according to His power, which mightily works within me.

Here, Paul used strong word pictures to communicate the blend of God's part and our part. His labor and our labor is manual labor, the kind of labor that produces sweat while working hard for long hours. But before the self-sufficient ones among us say, "See there, I told you that's the way the Christian life is supposed to work!" let's keep our respective fingers on the text. Paul describes his labor as *according to His power, which mightily works within me.* The power and wisdom of God gave Paul the strength and direction to do the will of God. He was not alone. Neither are we.

The Holy Spirit has been given to each believer to provide us with wisdom, insight, and divine strength. It is His power *which mightily works within* us to enable us to experience the unconditional love of God, the forgiveness that only God can give, and the strength to do His will even in the most difficult circumstances.

The Inherent Power of the Kingdom of God

Christ told many agrarian parables which illustrated the blend of our responsibility and God's enabling power. One of these is Mark 4:26-29:

...The kingdom of God is like a man who casts seed upon the soil; and goes to bed at night and gets up by day, and the seed sprouts up and grows—how, he himself does not know. The soil produces crops by itself; first the blade, then the head, then the mature grain in the head. But when the crop permits, he immediately puts in the sickle, because the harvest has come.

The farmer has an unmistakable responsibility in this process: He sows the seed, tends the soil, and harvests the grain. But the farmer cannot cause the seed to sprout and grow. The soil, not the farmer, *"produces crops by itself."* In his book, *The Parables of Jesus*, Simon Kistemaker wrote: "The farmer from the moment he has sown the seed must leave the sprouting, the growing, the pollinating, and the maturing to God. He can describe the process of growing wheat, but he cannot explain it."[2]

Whether this parable is applied to the seed of evangelism that will ultimately sprout, mature, and be harvested at the time of judgment, or more broadly to the truth of God sprouting and maturing in a person's life, the point is the same. God is the One who causes the growth (cf. 1 Cor. 3:7).

Codependent believers can take heart in this lesson. We are not alone. We are not left to our own devices to try to change our lives. The Lord is real and powerful and compassionate. He will act in our hearts and minds to change our perception of Him and of ourselves, but it will take time. Just as the farmer tilled the soil, sowed the seed, tended the crop, and harvested the mature grain, we have a limited responsibility to put ourselves in an environment that is conducive to the Lord's work in our lives. Then, like the farmer, we can expect Him to produce growth.

Suggestions and Questions

The following suggestions and questions may help you experience a balance of God's part and your part toward enjoying a changed life:

1. Be aware of cultural and personal pressures (e.g., codependency) that seem to force you to an extreme of self-sufficiency or hypermysticism.

2. Be honest. Where are you on the continuum? How do you live your life? Are you driven, passive, or balanced? Avoid the error of assuming that God is there only if you see signs and wonders. On the other hand, are you consistently tired, burned-out, burdened, too busy for the Lord, and unaware of His love and power? Is there any sense of excitement and mystery in your life (Mark 4:26-29), or is your life coldly rational and business-like?

3. Analyze your sources of input. How much television do you watch? Which shows, movies, or videos do you watch? What people do you spend time with? How do they influence you? What books are you reading? How much are you studying the Scriptures? (This analysis is not meant to be legalistic, but there are consequences for our choices.)

4. Spend time with people who experience the presence and the power of God, and who are balanced in their blend of responsibility and God's enabling. Who are some of these people? Where can you find someone like this?

5. Ask these questions regularly: What am I depending on God to do today? How can I enjoy the Lord today?

6. Ask God to reveal Himself to you so that you can experience His love and His power in your life. What is your responsibility in developing an intimate and powerful relationship with God? What is His responsibility?

Nineteen

Enjoying the Lord

Cathy had just moved to Dallas. She rented an apartment, got started in her new job, and then began looking for a church. She tried one for a few weeks and felt fairly comfortable there. The Sunday school class that she had attended was going to have a party. She went to it, thinking, *This will be a good way to get to know people.*

The party began with the usual stiffness that characterizes the gatherings of new people with others who have been long-time friends. For a while, Cathy felt like leaving. Few people initiated conversations with her. Then she found herself with a group of people who were also relatively new to Dallas. They talked about the business climate and the Dallas Cowboys. As the conversation continued, a man who had attended a Christian seminar began talking about the Lord. He was learning about the love of Christ, he explained. Cathy was interested. Then the man said, "The speaker at this seminar asked us, 'In what ways do you enjoy your relationship with God?' I thought that was a good question. Cathy, how would you answer that?"

Cathy tried to think of some way to end the conversation—gracefully and quickly! Could she tell them that she had forgotten about her appointment to have her nails done; that there were clothes in the dryer that would wrinkle if she didn't get them out; that she was expecting a phone call?

The group waited for her answer.

The problem for Cathy was that she didn't enjoy her relationship with the Lord. It was strictly business. Her father had been a stern businessman, and he treated his family the same way, looking for the bottom line in performance. There was very little warmth and affirmation in her relationship with him. Cathy assumed that the Lord was like her father: harsh, demanding, and aloof. She felt responsible for doing everything right, but guilty because she didn't. She lived under a cloud of assuming that God might tolerate her, but He certainly wasn't happy with her.

"En...enjoy my relationship with God?" she stammered.

"Yes," they replied, continuing to wait.

Not wanting to appear less than spiritual, Cathy figured out what to say and said it confidently, "Oh, I enjoy my devotional times. They are consistent and rich. I get so much out of them." Whew, that was over! The question went on to someone else.

There was truth in Cathy's statement. Her devotional life was consistent: consistently dry. And rich? That was a lie, unless you call introspection and self-condemnation *rich*. And yes, she got a lot out of them. She had marked every command she could find because she felt that if she fulfilled those, God would love her. She could explain the doctrine of grace almost as well as Martin Luther because she had become a driven student of the Scriptures, but her life was cold, dry, and Pharisaic. Enjoying the Lord was not in her repertoire of spiritual experiences.

The Shorter Version of the Westminster Catechism states succinctly: "The chief end of man is to glorify God and enjoy Him forever." Enjoying the Lord is not reserved for the hypermystics or the people who aren't in touch with the real hurts and pains of life. It is for anyone in the midst of the reality of life, because the presence of a living and powerful Savior is the ultimate reality that can give hope and purpose to every activity and circumstance. Codependents can learn that the Lord is not harsh and aloof. He is loving, strong, and wise. We can enjoy our relationship with Him.

A Snapshot from David's Life

The Psalms give us pictures of the psalmists' relationship with the Lord. There is very little fluff there. Instead, these men wrote and sang of the love, anger, and confusion that they felt. Psalm 27 gives us a snapshot from David's life. It shows the intimacy and faith of a man who has a grasp of the awesome love and strength of God. His perception is instructive for those of us who have difficulty with our perception of God. A study of the entire psalm would be helpful, but we will focus on the first four verses, with an emphasis on verse four:

> *The LORD is my light and my salvation; whom shall I fear? The LORD is the defense of my life; whom shall I dread? When evildoers came upon me to devour my flesh, my adversaries and my enemies, they stumbled and fell. Though a host encamp against me, my heart will not fear; though war arise against me, in spite of this I shall be confident. One thing I have asked from the LORD, that I shall seek: that I may dwell in the house of the LORD all the days of my life, to behold the beauty of the LORD, and to meditate in His temple.*

Let's take a closer look at verse four. David wrote, *One thing I have asked from the Lord, that I shall seek.* David was the king. He had many pressing responsibilities and countless headaches, yet he had a singleness of purpose. Like Mary in Luke 10:38-42, David saw the priority for intimacy and companionship with the Lord. That relationship was his highest priority in his busy life.

How did David describe the priority of his relationship with the Lord? He wrote, *...that I may dwell in the house of the Lord all the days of my life, to behold the beauty of the Lord...* In the Old Testament, the presence of God was in the temple, *the house of the Lord,* in the Holy of Holies. When Christ died on the cross, the veil of the temple was ripped from top to bottom (Matt. 27:51), and the presence of God was made available to all believers. The phrase, *to behold the beauty of the Lord,* can also be translated, *to behold the delightfulness of the Lord.* The Scriptures and the saints who have known the Lord intimately declare that the Lord is kind and strong, tender and powerful, protective and providing, warm, awesome, and creative. His wrath is very real, but it was paid by the blood of Christ, so that, *There is therefore now no condemnation for those who are in Christ Jesus* (Rom. 8:1). Is He delightful to you today? Do you enjoy Him, or do you believe that He only tolerates you? The idea that God only tolerates us isn't too delightful, is it?

David went on to say that he *meditates* about the delightfulness and beauty of the Lord. No, David wasn't an advocate of yoga or transcendental meditation. He simply meant that he took the time to think, to reflect, to ponder the character of God and his relationship with God. As our view of God becomes more accurate, we will find our thoughts drifting to Him much like an engaged couple whose thoughts drift toward each other. We can have that kind of intimacy and enjoyment in our relationship with the Lord! But then, why don't most of us have this kind of relationship with God?

Hindrances

The most obvious obstacle to a strong relationship with God is a wrong view of God. In our culture, we have lost the picture of the awesome nature of God. In the nineteenth century, people often spoke of God as "the Almighty." They had a great reverence for God. Twentieth-century technology has made us believe that we can provide for ourselves. We don't need God. In addition, humanism has eroded our clear theology of the depravity of man, the nature of creation, and the character of God. We are left, in our day, with a nice, but not too awe-inspiring figure of Christ. He has slipped in our minds from "the Almighty" to "Jesus, our friend." He certainly is our friend, but He is an awesome friend, more than just a little better and stronger than us. In C.S. Lewis's, *The Chronicles of Narnia*, the lion, Aslan, is the Christ figure. At critical points when the children were pondering Aslan's character, one of them would say, "Aslan is not a tame lion." Indeed, Christ is not tame and docile. He is our friend, but He is powerful, inscrutable, and majestic.

Many of us have also lost the picture of intimacy with God, and have settled for the structure of the Christian life. We live by commands and rules, structuring our lives to be "good Christians," but knowing very little of the warmth and intimacy that is ours to experience. The Scriptures contain a multitude of examples of the love and tenderness of God: Jesus welcomed the children to come sit and talk with Him so that He could affirm them (Matt. 19:13-15). The father of the prodigal son demonstrated the complete forgiveness of God as he wept for joy over his son's return. He then reinstated him into the family with full honors (Luke 15:11-32). Paul describes our reconciliation with God. He says that we were enemies of God, but He has made us His friends (Col. 1:19-22; Rom. 5:6-11). In Eph. 1:5; Gal. 4:6; and Rom. 8:15, he states that we who were hopeless and helpless have been adopted as God's beloved children.

Some of us think that God is disgusted with us because we have let Him down so often. This perceived alienation makes us very reluctant to ask Him for things. We can be encouraged by Christ's affirmation:

> *Or what man is there among you, when his son shall ask him for a loaf, will give him a stone? Or if he shall ask for a fish, he will not give him a snake, will he? If you then being evil, know how to give good gifts to your children, how much more shall your Father who is in heaven give what is good to those who ask Him!* Matt. 7:9-11

An inaccurate view of God leads to numerous other hindrances in our relationship with God. We develop wrong goals by pursuing success, pleasure, and the approval of others in a vain attempt to fill the void in our lives. We shift into a performance mode, valuing or devaluing ourselves by how much we do. We are driven to accomplish as much as possible to prove our worth, or we give up and become passive, hoping nobody will notice us. Some of us become extremely analytical, trying to figure out how we can be better, how to get others to appreciate us, and how to avoid mistakes of the past. Healthy analysis is good, but this kind of analysis isn't healthy. It leads to morbid introspection and self-condemnation.

An inaccurate view of God leaves us alone, blinded, weak, driven, numb, or some combination of these—a far cry from enjoying the Lord and living a strong, intimate, secure, and honest Christian life.

Suggestions and Questions

1. Be honest. One night, Joyce and I talked about our perceptions of God, and in the middle of the discussion, she said, "You don't really believe that God loves you; do you?" She had me. I decided to be honest, and that honesty was the beginning of a long and positive change in my view of God.

   a) What are some characteristics of the most delightful relationships you have ever had?

   b) In what ways do you enjoy the Lord?

c) What factors hinder you from enjoying the Lord more fully?

d) What can you do about them?

2. Ask God to change your view of Him.

  a) Paraphrase these passages:

Ps. 27:1-4

> *The LORD is my light and my salvation; whom shall I fear?*
> *The LORD is the defense of my life; whom shall I dread?*
> *When evildoers came upon me to devour my flesh, my*
> *adversaries and my enemies, they stumbled and fell.*
> *Though a host encamp against me, my heart will not fear;*
> *though war arise against me, in spite of this I shall be*
> *confident. One thing I have asked from the LORD, that I*
> *shall seek: that I may dwell in the house of the LORD all*
> *the days of my life, to behold the beauty of the LORD, and*
> *to meditate in His temple.*

Paraphrase:

Ps. 16:11

> *Thou wilt make known to me the path of life; in Thy*
> *presence is fulness of joy; in Thy right hand there are*
> *pleasures forever.*

Paraphrase:

Luke 10:38-42

Now as they were traveling along, He entered a certain village; and a woman named Martha welcomed Him into her home. And she had a sister called Mary, who moreover was listening to the Lord's word, seated at His feet. But Martha was distracted with all her preparations; and she came up to Him, and said, "Lord, do You not care that my sister has left me to do all the serving alone? Then tell her to help me." But the Lord answered and said to her, "Martha, Martha, you are worried and bothered about so many things; but only a few things are necessary, really only one, for Mary has chosen the good part, which shall not be taken away from her."

Paraphrase:

Hosea 6:3

So let us know, let us press on to know the LORD. His going forth is as certain as the dawn; and He will come to us like the rain, like the spring rain watering the earth.

Paraphrase:

b) Describe how your view of God might change. Include all three elements of the process: cognitive, relational, and mystical.

3. Delight yourself in the Lord. How can you enjoy the Lord more today?

Twenty

Three Stages of Growth

When a person learns about the effects of his codependency and begins to experience the healing process, all kinds of changes take place. His view of God and his perception of himself change. His relationships, values, priorities, and his lifestyle change. An understanding of the stages of growth helps us realize that the awkwardness of change doesn't mean we are going crazy! It means we are growing!

Describing the Three Stages

The three stages of growth are: rules-oriented, adolescence, and relationship-oriented.[1] Codependents are almost universally in the rules-oriented stage until they begin to identify their codependent behavior, detach to reflect, and decide to make their own choices. This triggers the grief process. Anger and grieving are the beginnings of adolescence. Then they begin to move farther through the awkward stage of adolescence, which is characterized by excesses in behavior and confusion. After progressing through this awkward phase of growth, codependents can then move into the freedom and enjoyment of a relationship-oriented life.

The following integrates these steps and stages; let's take a look at some characteristics of each stage:

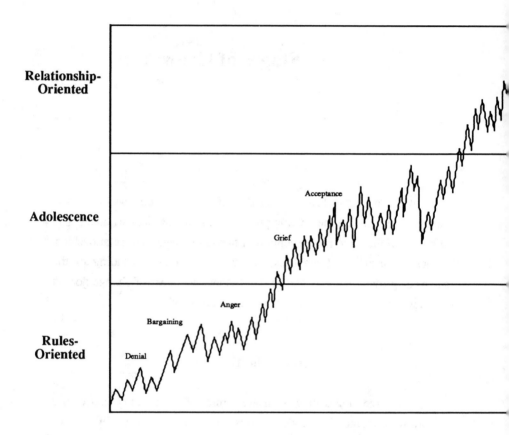

Rules-Oriented:

rigid adherence to structure and form

do's and don'ts

well-defined set of acceptable activities and habits

expecting everyone to respond in the same way

tendency to look for formulas

uncomfortable with ambiguity

looking for a guaranteed outcome

anger or confusion when simple answers aren't given

pride in strengths; denial or hypersensitivity to weaknesses

intense desire to please others and accomplish tasks

lack of objectivity

comparison, guilt, loneliness, introspection

repressed emotions

driven or passive

feelings easily hurt, defensive

serving to gain approval

pat answers

emphasis on accountability and control

Adolescence:

awkwardness in the midst of change

confusion because rules aren't working

experimenting with breaking rules

new sense of freedom and honesty

rebellion, depression, enthusiasm

excesses in emotions, language, and behavior

repressed anger emerges

new friends

risks of isolation

Relationship-Oriented:

enjoying the Lord and people

honest, objective, mature, secure

comfortable with ambiguity

few simple answers

obedience out of gratitude

freedom to be one's self, no comparison

freedom to let people be themselves

less afraid of weaknesses

> less prideful of strengths
> focus on faithfulness, not success
> serving out of appreciation
> able to let people fail and still affirm them

Many of us would like to think that we are farther along in the process than we actually are. One man told me, "I must be in the adolescent stage because I have been angry and hurt several times." Objectivity had not yet penetrated this man's life. He was still defensive and driven to please others with his accomplishments. He was squarely in the rules stage.

Many codependents and others in the rules-oriented stage define "maturity" as the upper end of the rules stage; that is, being able to live by rules as effectively as possible. The idea of struggling with adolescent issues is seen as immaturity, rebellion, and sin, not progress.

In the adolescent stage, some of the deeply held convictions of the rules stage are overturned and replaced by their opposite in excess. A person who has repressed his emotions may believe that all of his feelings are good and right. "I can trust how I feel," he might say, "because my emotions are a part of me." Another who has had a rigidly disciplined life may become very disorganized and irresponsible. Someone who has "served" tirelessly, but to please people, may completely withdraw from service when he realizes what his motives have been. There are all kinds of extremes in the emotional adolescent stage, just as there are many excesses in the physical adolescent stage. (A visit to a local high school might give you some perception about excesses in adolescence!) But adolescence is not death! It is a part of the process of growth and maturity; an essential part. Those of us who enter that awkward stage need affirmation and perception, not condemnation.

Why Are We Afraid of the Adolescent Stage?

Most of us are afraid of the adolescent stage. Similar to our desire to skip the anger phase of the grief process, we want to skip the adolescent stage and move on to maturity. Life, however, doesn't work that way.

Adolescence is confusing. It's awkward. It often seems like we aren't making any progress. In fact, it seems like we're going backward, not forward! As changes occur, we find ourselves feeling emotions we have seldom felt, saying things we have never said before, and doing things we have always considered wrong. We don't recognize ourselves anymore! What if other people think we're weird?!?

I heard a mother say about her thirteen-year-old son, "I wish I could lock him in a room until he is twenty-one. I don't know if I can stand his adolescent years!" Many of us feel the same way about our emotional adolescence (or someone else's!). We wish we could take a maturity pill or go to sleep and wake up after adolescence is over. But we have to go through the process, even though it is awkward and difficult.

If we look into the adolescent swamp and decide not to go through it, the effects will be far more devastating than anything we fear in adolescence. Our guilt motivation will become hardened. We will continue to be driven until we burn out, or we will become increasingly numb in our passivity. There is a certain safety in staying in the rules-oriented status quo, but it is comparable to the safety of staying in an airplane that is going to crash. The perception of safety is only a temporary illusion.

Affirming People in the Process

People who are entering the adolescent stage need an environment that will help them assimilate all of their many conflicting thoughts and feelings. They need a friend who will patiently listen and understand. They don't need quick and easy answers, nor do they need to be told that they are "carnal" unless they are choosing a pattern of sin. As any parent of a teenager can tell you, this is a very difficult stage because one doesn't know where to draw the line and where to give freedom. Most codependents have drawn the line much too near a rigid, rules-dominated lifestyle all of their lives. Any change will seem like abject rebellion to some of them. They need to be affirmed and encouraged in the process, not bludgeoned back into rigidity by calloused condemnation.

Barb was on the verge of making some major discoveries. While teaching a Bible study on grace, she realized that she had been living by rigid rules. Over a period of a month or so, as she and a friend began to study the grace of God, she began to sense the freedom and intimacy she had been teaching about! Her inspiration began to change from a "have-to" to a "want-to" motivation. After church one day, she excitedly told her Sunday school teacher about her new revelations. His response was, "You're taking this too far, Barb. If people believed what you're talking about, we couldn't get anybody to do anything around here. I don't want to put a damper on your enthusiasm (*sure!*), but I don't want you to tell anybody in the class about this, okay?"

Barb was dumbfounded. She hadn't expected him to burst into "The Hallelujah Chorus," but she *had* expected him to be positive at least! His self-righteous condemnation crushed her. It was months before she felt confident in her new freedom and joy again.

Buddy had a different experience. When he learned about his codependency, he began to experience emotions he had never felt before. His friends and family had always expected him to be the model of Christian virtue, and he had tried very hard to meet those expectations. He had pleased them, rescued them, and in the process, had repressed his own desires and emotions. Now, however, those emotions were emerging, and some of them weren't very pleasant! A good friend, Ray, met with him regularly during this time, and Buddy felt free to say what was on his mind. At first, Buddy was surprised that Ray didn't tell him to "shape up." He was even more surprised as Ray listened, asked questions, and seemed to value his opinions even though they seemed so new and strange. Ray rarely corrected Buddy's ideas. He allowed Buddy to go through the awkwardness of adolescence and gave him affirmation and understanding. In that environment, Buddy developed a sense of reality about the good and bad of life. The months and years passed. Ray and Buddy developed a unique friendship, and many others benefited from the wisdom and security of their relationship.

Where Are You in the Process?

Don't despair if you see yourself as a rules-oriented person. The fact that you accurately perceive your rigidity is an important step toward maturity. If you are getting in touch with your codependency and experiencing anger and grief, you may be entering adolescence. Maybe you have been in the awkwardness of adolescence for some time, and you are wondering what's wrong with you. And maybe some of you have progressed into maturity.

Wherever you are in the process, be content there. You don't have to be farther along to be acceptable! Growth will come if you put yourself in a positive, understanding environment. The reason this chapter is included is not to force people to hurry through the process, but to help you understand that there is all kinds of strangeness and excessiveness in the life of a codependent person who is entering adolescence. If you understand this and learn to anticipate the extremes, adolescence may not be quite so weird!

Questions

1. Why are codependents almost universally in the rules-oriented stage (at least until they begin to be objective)?

2. Where are you in the process? How can you tell?

3. Are you afraid of adolescence? Why, or why not?

4. What (or who) do you need to help you continue plodding through the process?

Twenty-One

Waiting on the Lord

Stephanie's husband called me one night recently. Though she had heard about codependency for some time, he told me, she had just realized the week before that her family was dysfunctional and that she had been deeply affected by them. "She was really excited," he reported. "She suddenly saw those six characteristics of codependency in her life, and then started reading about codependency during every spare minute. She was amazed that she hadn't seen it before! But a couple of days ago, she remembered some things that happened to her when she was a child. She started crying, and she didn't stop for two hours. While she was crying, she thought of several more things that her parents had done to her sister and her."

"How is she doing now?" I asked.

"After all of that, she realized that she relates to her boss at work in the same way that she related to her father. She withdraws from him, feels terrible and guilty, and then she gets really confused around him."

"So she's not doing too well, I take it."

"No, she's not. She was so excited last week, but so depressed this week. What's going on?" he asked.

Stephanie's initial understanding of her codependency had been full of excitement and hope: *Maybe, just maybe, this will explain why I feel and act like I do!* Her growing objectivity, however, brought back pain that had been hidden for years, and its crushing weight overwhelmed her. Hope turned to despair.

Perhaps this has happened to you as you have read through these pages. You may have experienced the joy of discovery only to find that what you discovered is a monster! You may have vacillated several times between hope and despair, between euphoria and depression. (That would be like a codependent, wouldn't it!?)

David's honesty carried him from the top of the wave to the bottom many times. The Psalms reflect his up-and-down emotions—an honest reflection of a real person observing real life. There was a benchmark in David's life, however; a benchmark that he always came back to sooner or later. That benchmark was the love, wisdom, and power of God. It gave him a tenacious hope in the middle of great trauma in his life. We have looked at the first several verses of Psalm 27 in this book. Now we will examine the last several verses. (The middle ones aren't bad either!) David didn't gloss over the reality of his situations or the pain he felt, but kept his eyes on the character of God.

> *Teach me Thy way, O LORD, and lead me in a level path, because of my foes. Do not deliver me over to the desire of my adversaries; for false witnesses have risen against me, and such as breathe out violence. I would have despaired unless I had believed that I would see the goodness of the LORD in the land of the living. Wait for the Lord; be strong, and let your heart take courage; yes, wait for the LORD.*
>
> Ps. 27:11-14

If he had not believed that he would see God work in his circumstances, he would have despaired. When he began to lose hope, when he began to feel that he couldn't make it and that God had left him alone, he riveted his attention on the goodness of God. The Lord might work quickly. He might not. He might work without having David do a thing, or David's laborious participation might be an integral part of the solution. But somehow, God would work, and David would see His goodness.

With that sense of confidence, David instructs his listeners to *wait for the Lord; be strong, and let your heart take courage; yes, wait for the Lord.*

How certain can we be that God will work in our circumstances? Another psalm says that we can be as sure of God's gracious intervention as we are that the sun will come up:

> *I wait for the LORD, my soul does wait, and in His word do I hope. My soul waits for the Lord more than the watchmen for the morning; indeed, more than the watchmen for the morning.* Ps. 130:5-6

I had an experience years ago that gave me a little insight into this passage. Between our junior and senior years in college, my friend Graham Thorpe and I headed West after working for most of the summer. We had planned the trip for months, pouring over maps and planning our routes so we could see everything we possibly could in four weeks. We threw our sleeping bags, an old tent, and a Coleman stove in the back of my mother's car. Then we went to the Piggly Wiggly in Macon, Georgia, to buy the necessities for the trip. We were really into health food: coffee, field peas, bread, and Vienna sausage.

We drove to Arkansas to see Graham's grandmother. Then we drove on to Arizona where we hiked to the bottom of the Grand Canyon and back in a day (The ranger said we shouldn't try that. He was right!). We spent a few days in Las Vegas, a week with friends in Los Angeles, a week camping up the coast of California, a day in Muir Woods, and then we headed for the high point of the trip, literally and figuratively, Mount Whitney.

At 14,496 feet, Mount Whitney is the highest mountain in the Continental United States. After a night at the beginning of the trail, we filled our packs and headed up the mountain. It was a gorgeous day on a spectacular trail! Movie Flats (where many old westerns were filmed) came into view as we climbed. We passed through huge fir trees before they shrank to gnarled nubs at the timberline. We passed Guitar Lake, and finally, we came to our stopping point for the day, creatively named "Trail Camp."

Graham and I made camp and then enjoyed a tasty and nourishing meal of field peas, Vienna sausage, bread, and water from our canteen. (Joyce still can't believe we ate that stuff.) We remarked that it was exciting for two Georgians to camp so close to a snow bank (we called it *a glacier*) in mid-September. It had been a long day. Tired, we got in our sleeping bags at about seven o' clock to be ready for an early start the next morning.

The night was a little cooler than I had planned for. I woke up at eight o' clock (in the evening!) shivering uncontrollably. My old Boy Scout sleeping bag was perfectly suitable for a place like Rainey Mountain in North Georgia, but it was good for only about 45 degrees. It was decidedly colder than that at 12,000 feet on the side of Mount Whitney! Graham, the rat, was asleep.

I scrunched up in a ball to conserve what little warmth I could muster, and for the next several months (okay, so it was hours), I tried to keep my mind off of the eminent probability of frost bite and amputation by watching the fabulous show of stars in the cloudless night sky. The many shooting stars were, however, small consolation for impending dismemberment...or so it seemed.

At about three o' clock in the morning, I glanced toward the east, just to see if the sun might make a surprise appearance. No luck. From that point on, I kept an eye on the eastern horizon, waiting for the first rays to appear. I figured that the odds were definitely in my favor; the sun had come up every day since creation! It was just a matter of time. The hours passed painfully slowly, and as 4:30 came and went, my tension was mounting. I was certain the sun would come up, but when?!? I was getting so tired of waiting. I had seen all the stars I wanted to see for the rest of my life!

At about 5:15, either somebody in Omaha lit a candle, or the first glimmer of the sun's rays appeared on the horizon. It was so dim that it could have been either one. But that was good enough for me! I shot out of my sleeping bag (which, by now, I figured had its own hidden refrigeration system), and said, "Come on, Graham, the sun's up! It's time to go!" Graham rolled over, looked up at the still black sky and mumbled, "You're crazy. It's still night."

"Look over there," I pointed eastward. "See, the sun's up. Let's go!" Graham looked at me like I had lost any semblance of sanity, but he must have thought that I was beyond reason. He got up, we grabbed another nutritious bite, and started up to the top of Whitney. (To be honest, it was kind of hard to see the trail because it was still so dark! But I wouldn't admit that to Graham.)

Waiting for the dawn had been hard, but my sense of certainty had given me hope and confidence. In the same way, we can be certain that if we have trusted the Lord, He will work in our lives. The wait may be long and hard, but that sureness gives us hope and confidence to endure.

Many of us want complete relief from the painful effects of codependency, and we want it now! Phil is a friend of mine who expects some divine revelation or cataclysmic event to move him instantly from his codependency to perfect health and wholeness (which none of us can experience until we go to be with the Lord). He said, "I keep waiting for the bubble to pop and for everything to be what it ought to be." That's an unrealistic expectation. We may have periodic flashes of insight, but the grind of growth is always slow. The sky doesn't instantly turn from pitch black to noon. It is much more gradual than that. First, there are glimmers of light that are so faint one wonders if it is light at all. Then, more light appears before the actual sunrise bursts above the horizon and begins to take the chill out of the air. Several more hours pass before the warmth of the sun is felt to a significant degree. Our spiritual and emotional growth is very much like that: slow, gradual, and certain, if we are in a positive environment. It will not happen suddenly, but it will happen.

Also, just as the light of the sun reveals those things that have been hidden in darkness, the light of objectivity reveals more wounds and hurts in us. Increased objectivity eventually brings healing, but it also brings more pain for a while. Don't think that you are regressing. You are, to use a previously given metaphor, peeling off another layer of the onion. Each layer contains new revelations, new insights, new pain, and new healing. That's progress.

When the watchman waited for the dawn, he was not passive. His job was to warn the city in case of attack. He was watching for the enemy. He had to be prepared, active, and sharp in his observations and readiness to act. Our waiting on the Lord isn't to be passive, either. We are responsible to be prepared, to be observant, and to be active in the defense of our lives against the attacks of our enemies: denial, being a savior or a Judas, being easily manipulated, manipulating others, hurt, destructive anger, guilt, and loneliness.

For many of us, the night of codependency has been long. We're tired of waiting, and we're on the verge of despair. We may have thought that we saw some rays of dawn, but it may have been wishful thinking. Or, we may have actually seen those rays, but we were expecting an instant noon, not a gradual dawning. And we are discouraged.

Don't give up! Don't expect too much too soon, but do expect the Lord to work in your life: slowly, patiently, and certainly. He cares for you more than you can imagine, and He is full of wisdom and strength. You can be sure that His light will outshine the darkness of your codependency, and that He will bring you healing, hope, and health.

So let us know, let us press on to know the LORD. His going forth is as certain as the dawn; and He will come to us like the rain, like the spring rain watering the earth.

Hosea 6:3

Questions

1. What discourages you most about the process of combatting codependency?

2. Describe what it means to *wait for the Lord.* How could that help you?

3. Describe some realistic expectations of a gradual "dawning" of independence, intimacy, and health in your life:

4. Now that you have finished this book, what will be your next step? (Possibly: Go through the book and answer the questions again at a deeper level, or go through the material and questions with a friend.)

Appendixes A-F

Introduction

The following exercises are designed to help you analyze how your family has shaped your view of God and affected both your self-concept and your relationships with others. These exercises cover some of the same ground in different ways; however, most of us have a great need for objectivity. It is our hope that these exercises will provide you with more insight and perception by looking at similar issues from a variety of angles.[*]

---

[*]Appendixes A-F are reprinted and adapted from *Your Parents and You* by permission (Houston and Dallas, TX: Rapha Publishing/Word, Inc., 1990), pp. 191-221.

Evaluating Your Relationship

with Your Father

On the next page is an exercise to help you evaluate your relationship between you and your father as you were growing up. Check the appropriate square as you recall how he related to you when you were young. Here's an example:

Characteristics	Always	Very often	Some- times	Hardly Ever	Never	Don't Know
Gentle			✔			
Stern	✔					
Loving			✔			
Aloof			✔			
Disapproving		✔				

WHEN I WAS A CHILD, MY FATHER WAS...

Characteristics	Always	Very often	Some-times	Hardly Ever	Never	Don't Know
Gentle						
Stern						
Loving						
Aloof						
Disapproving						
Distant						
Close and Intimate						
Kind						
Angry						
Caring						
Demanding						
Interested						
Discipliner						
Gracious						
Harsh						
Wise						
Holy						
Leader						
Provider						
Trustworthy						
Joyful						
Forgiving						
Good						
Cherishing of Me						
Compassionate						
Impatient						
Unreasonable						
Strong						
Protective						
Passive						
Encouraging						
Sensitive						
Just						
Unpredictable						

Evaluation of Your Relationship
with Your Father

1. What does this inventory tell you about your relationship with your father?

_____

_____

_____

_____

_____

_____

_____

_____

_____

_____

2. If you were an objective observer of the type of relationship you have just described, how would you feel about the father?

_____

_____

_____

_____

_____

_____

_____

_____

_____

_____

3. About the child?

_____
_____
_____
_____
_____
_____
_____

4. How would you respond to the father? Be specific.

_____
_____
_____
_____
_____
_____
_____

5. To the child?

_____
_____
_____
_____
_____
_____

Evaluating Your Relationship
with Your Mother

Now complete the same exercise to evaluate your relationship with your *mother* as you were growing up.

Characteristics	Always	Very often	Some- times	Hardly Ever	Never	Don't Know
Gentle			✔			
Stern	✔					
Loving			✔			
Aloof			✔			
Disapproving		✔				

WHEN I WAS A CHILD, MY MOTHER WAS...

Characteristics	Always	Very often	Some-times	Hardly Ever	Never	Don't Know
Gentle		✓				
Stern		✓				
Loving	✓					
Aloof				✓		
Disapproving				✓		
Distant					✓	
Close and Intimate		✓				
Kind					✓	
Angry				✓		
Caring	✓					
Demanding		✓				
Interested	✓					
Discipliner		✓				
Gracious	✓					
Harsh					✓	
Wise	✓					
Holy			✓			
Leader		✓				
Provider		✓				
Trustworthy		✓				
Joyful		✓				
Forgiving		✓				
Good	✓					
Cherishing of Me	✓					
Compassionate	✓					
Impatient				✓		
Unreasonable					✓	
Strong		✓				
Protective			✓			
Passive					✓	
Encouraging	✓					
Sensitive	✓					
Just		✓				
Unpredictable					✓	

Evaluation of Your Relationship
with Your Mother

1. What does this inventory tell you about your relationship with your mother?

   _____

   _____

   _____

   _____

   _____

   _____

   _____

   _____

   _____

   _____

2. If you were an objective observer of the type of relationship you have just described, how would you feel about the mother?

   _____

   _____

   _____

   _____

   _____

   _____

   _____

   _____

   _____

   _____

3. About the child?

_____

_____

_____

_____

_____

_____

_____

_____

4. How would you respond to the mother? Be specific.

_____

_____

_____

_____

_____

_____

_____

5. To the child?

_____

_____

_____

_____

_____

_____

_____

Evaluating Your
Relationship with God

This inventory is designed to help you evaluate your relationship with God. Because it is subjective, there are no right or wrong answers. To ensure that the test reveals your actual feelings, please follow the instructions carefully.

1. Answer openly and honestly. Don't respond from a theological knowledge of God, but from personal experience.

2. Don't describe what the relationship *ought* to be, or what you hope it *will be*, but what it *is* right now.

3. Some people feel God might be displeased if they give a negative answer. Nothing is further from the truth. He is pleased with our honesty. A foundation of transparency is required for growth to occur.

4. Turn each characteristic into a question. For example: *To what degree do I really feel God loves me? To what degree do I really feel that God understands me?*

5. As you respond, try to recall times of stress and difficulty, as well as normal situations.

TO WHAT DEGREE DO I REALLY FEEL GOD IS...

Characteristics	Always	Very often	Some-times	Hardly Ever	Never	Don't Know
Gentle						
Stern						
Loving						
Aloof						
Disapproving						
Distant						
Close and Intimate						
Kind						
Angry						
Caring						
Demanding						
Interested						
Discipliner						
Gracious						
Harsh						
Wise						
Holy						
Leader						
Provider						
Trustworthy						
Joyful						
Forgiving						
Good						
Cherishing of Me						
Compassionate						
Impatient						
Unreasonable						
Strong						
Protective						
Passive						
Encouraging						
Sensitive						
Just						
Unpredictable						

Evaluation of Your Relationship with God

1. What does this exercise tell you about your relationship with God?

_____

_____

_____

_____

_____

_____

_____

_____

_____

2. Are there any differences between what you know (theologically) and how you feel (emotionally) about Him? If so, what are they?

_____

_____

_____

_____

_____

_____

_____

_____

_____

Appendix D

Your Father's Influence
on Your Perception of God

How has your relationship with your father influenced your perception of your heavenly Father? To get a comparison, transfer all the check marks you made for your father on page 266 to the *shaded columns* on page 278. Use a check mark for this category.

When you have completed this, transfer the check marks you made on page 274 which relate to your relationship with God. To make them more obvious, use an "✗" for this category. Put them in the *white columns* in the appropriate places.

Characteristics	Always	Very often	Some-times	Hardly Ever	Never	Don't Know
Gentle		✗	✔			
Stern	✔	✗				
Loving		✗	✔			
Aloof		✔		✗		
Disapproving			✔			

Instructions: Transfer all check marks from page 266 to the SHADED columns.
Transfer all check marks from page 274 to the WHITE columns.

Characteristics	Always	Very often	Some-times	Hardly Ever	Never	Don't Know
Gentle						
Stern						
Loving						
Aloof						
Disapproving						
Distant						
Close and Intimate						
Kind						
Angry						
Caring						
Demanding						
Interested						
Discipliner						
Gracious						
Harsh						
Wise						
Holy						
Leader						
Provider						
Trustworthy						
Joyful						
Forgiving						
Good						
Cherishing of Me						
Compassionate						
Impatient						
Unreasonable						
Strong						
Protective						
Passive						
Encouraging						
Sensitive						
Just						
Unpredictable						

What Did You Learn?

1. Which characteristics are the same for both your father and your heavenly Father?

_____

_____

_____

_____

_____

_____

_____

_____

_____

_____

2. Which characteristics are quite different (two or more boxes away from each other)?

_____

_____

_____

_____

_____

_____

_____

_____

_____

3. What patterns (if any) do you see?

_____

_____

_____

_____

_____

_____

_____

_____

_____

4. Write a summary paragraph about how your perception of God has been shaped by your relationship with your father:

_____

_____

_____

_____

_____

_____

_____

_____

_____

_____

_____

_____

_____

_____

_____

Your Mother's Influence
on Your Perception of God

How has your mother influenced your perception of your heavenly Father? To get a comparison, transfer all the check marks you made for your mother on page 270 to the *shaded columns* on page 282. Use a check mark for this category.

When you have completed this, transfer the check marks you made on page 274 which relate to your relationship with God. To make them more obvious, use an "**✗**" for this category. Put them in the *white columns* in the appropriate places.

Characteristics	Always	Very often	Some-times	Hardly Ever	Never	Don't Know
Gentle		✗	✔			
Stern	✔	✗				
Loving		✗	✔			
Aloof		✔		✗		
Disapproving			✔			

Instructions: Transfer all check marks from page 270 to the SHADED columns.
Transfer all check marks from page 274 to the WHITE columns.

Characteristics	Always	Very often	Some-times	Hardly Ever	Never	Don't Know
Gentle						
Stern						
Loving						
Aloof						
Disapproving						
Distant						
Close and Intimate						
Kind						
Angry						
Caring						
Demanding						
Interested						
Discipliner						
Gracious						
Harsh						
Wise						
Holy						
Leader						
Provider						
Trustworthy						
Joyful						
Forgiving						
Good						
Cherishing of Me						
Compassionate						
Impatient						
Unreasonable						
Strong						
Protective						
Passive						
Encouraging						
Sensitive						
Just						
Unpredictable						

What Did You Learn?

1. Which characteristics are the same for both your mother and your heavenly Father?

_____

_____

_____

_____

_____

_____

_____

_____

2. Which characteristics are quite different (two or more boxes away from each other)?

_____

_____

_____

_____

_____

_____

_____

_____

3. What patterns (if any) do you see?

_____

_____

_____

_____

_____

_____

_____

_____

4. Write a summary paragraph about how your perception of God has
   been shaped by your relationship with your mother:

_____

_____

_____

_____

_____

_____

_____

_____

_____

_____

_____

_____

_____

_____

_____

_____

_____

Appendix F

Analyzing Your Family

This exercise will help you remember what the relationships in your family were like as you were growing up and how you have been affected by them.

Check the appropriate box or write your responses to the following questions:

1. How would you describe your parent's marriage?
   - ❏ Unhappy
   - ❏ Poor
   - ❏ Good
   - ❏ Happy

2. Would you describe your home life as...
   - ❏ Unhappy
   - ❏ Poor
   - ❏ Good
   - ❏ Happy

3. Would you describe your father as:

❏ Passive	❏ Gregarious	❏ Angry	❏ Sad	❏ Other
❏ Strong	❏ Gentle	❏ Harsh	❏ Loving	❏ Manipulative

4. Did your father take time to play with you and your brothers and/or sisters? ❑ Yes ❑ No

5. Was your father...Dictatorial_____ Indifferent_____
   Interested in you_____ Open_____ Tender_____ Protective_____

6. How important was TV to your father?
   ❑ Addicted to it ❑ Occasional viewer ❑ Seldom/Never watched

7. Are you afraid of becoming like your father? ❑ Yes ❑ No
   Explain:

   _____

   _____

   _____

   _____

   _____

8. Would you describe your mother as:
   ❑ Passive ❑ Gregarious ❑ Angry ❑ Sad ❑ Other
   ❑ Strong ❑ Gentle ❑ Harsh ❑ Loving ❑ Manipulative

9. Did your mother take time to play with you and your brothers and/or sisters? ❑ Yes ❑ No

10. Was your mother...Dictatorial_____ Indifferent_____
    Interested in you_____ Open_____ Tender_____ Protective_____

11. How important was TV to your mother?
❑ Addicted to it   ❑ Occasional viewer   ❑ Seldom/Never watched

12. Are you afraid of becoming like your mother?   ❑ Yes   ❑ No
Explain:

_____

_____

_____

_____

_____

13. What did you enjoy doing the most as a child in a family setting?

_____

_____

_____

_____

_____

14. Did your father and mother argue...
    ❑ Frequently   ❑ Seldom   ❑ Never

15. *a*) Would you classify your parent's economic status as...
    ❑ Upper class   ❑ Middle class   ❑ Lower class

    b) What impact did this economic status have on you?

_____

_____

_____

16. Are your parents living now?
      Mother: ❑ Yes   ❑ No
      Father: ❑ Yes   ❑ No

17. *a*) Describe your relationship with your father:

_____

_____

_____

_____

_____

_____

   b) ...with your mother:

_____

_____

_____

_____

_____

_____

_____

18. *a*) Did your father demonstrate affection toward your mother?
      ❑ Yes   ❑ No

   If so, how? If not, why not?

_____

_____

_____

_____

b) Did your mother demonstrate affection toward your father?
❑ Yes   ❑ No

If so, how? If not, why not?

_____

_____

_____

_____

_____

19. Are you close to your brothers and sisters?
❑ Yes   ❑ No

Explain:

_____

_____

_____

_____

_____

20. *a*) Were you teased as a child?
❑ Yes   ❑ No

b) If yes, what about?

_____

_____

_____

_____

c) Who teased you the most?

_____

_____

_____

_____

d) What was your emotional response?

_____

_____

_____

_____

21. *a*) Were you ever sexually abused as a child by anyone in your family? Did anyone in your family ever look at you lustfully, tease you, touch you, or engage you in any type of behavior which exposed you to his or her sexuality?

    ❑ Yes ❑ No

    b) Did anyone else abuse you by exposing you to adult sexual feelings or behavior during your childhood?

    ❑ Yes ❑ No

    c) If you answered yes to either of the above questions, how has childhood sexual abuse affected you and your relationships with others, including God?

22. *a*) To your knowledge, was one or both of your parents sexually abused as a child?

    ❑ Yes ❑ No

    b) If so, how has this affected you and your relationships with others, including God?

_____

_____

_____

_____

_____

_____

_____

_____

_____

23. *a*) Did you try to manipulate your parents to get attention or special treatment?

❏ Yes   ❏ No

b) If so, how?

_____

_____

_____

_____

_____

24. *a*) Did your parents agree with each other on how to discipline you?

❏ Yes   ❏ No

b) Describe how you were disciplined when you were a child:

_____

_____

_____

25. *a*) Did you ever have any serious illness as a child?

❏ Yes   ❏ No

b) If so, how did this affect you and your relationship with your parents and siblings?

_____

_____

_____

26. Was there anything about you for which your parents communicated consistent disapproval? If so, what?

_____

_____

_____

27. *a)* Are there any periods of your life you cannot remember?
❑ Yes   ❑ No

b) If so, which period(s)?

_____

_____

_____

_____

_____

_____

28. Which parent did you enjoy being with the most as a child?
❑ Father   ❑ Mother

Why?

_____

_____

29. Has this exercise prompted any feelings in you about your home life? If so, describe them:

_____

_____

_____

_____

_____

_____

_____

Observations and Analysis

Imagine that you are a consultant in family relationships. You have just reviewed the answers written in Appendix F, and you are asked to give an impartial analysis to your professional colleagues about this family. Write out your conclusions:

1. What are the strengths of this family?

_____

_____

_____

_____

_____

2. What are some of the difficulties of this family?

_____

_____

_____

_____

_____

3. Describe the relationship of the husband and wife:

_____

_____

_____

_____

_____

_____

_____

_____

4. Describe the father's relationship with each child:

_____

_____

_____

_____

_____

5. Describe the mother's relationship with each child:

_____

_____

_____

_____

_____

6. How was the character of God modeled by these parents?

_____

_____

_____

_____

_____

_____

7. How was the character of God distorted by these parents?

_____

_____

_____

_____

_____

_____

_____

_____

Notes

Introduction
[1] Nicholi Armand, "Changes in the American Family: Their Impact on Individual Development and on Society," *Family Research Council*, p. 2. Reprint.

1. Glimpses
[1] Melody Beattie, *Codependent No More* (New York: Hazelden Foundation, 1987), p. 31.

2. The Cause of Codependency
[1] Armand, "Changes in the American Family," *Family Research Council*, p. 2.

[2] Beth Brophy, "Children Under Stress," *U.S. News & World Report*, Oct. 27, 1986, p. 63.

[3] *Ibid.*, p. 63.

[4] Anthony M. Casale, *USA Today: Tracking Tomorrow's Trends* (Kansas City: Andrews, McMeel and Parker, 1986), p. 111.

[5] Brophy, "Children Under Stress," *USN&WR*, Oct. 27, 1986.

[6] Richard Price, "Riding the Currents of the Culture." Topic presented at the annual retreat of campus directors of Campus Crusade for Christ, Nov., 1988.

[7] Burton White, *The First Three Years of Life*. Rev. Ed. (New York: Prentice-Hall Press, 1985), pp. 323-324.

4. A Warped Sense of Responsibility
[1] Claude M. Steiner, *Scripts People Live* (New York: Grove Press, 1974), as quoted by Melody Beattie, *Codependent No More*, p. 77.

5. Controlled/Controlling
[1] Charlotte Fedders and Laura Elliot, *Shattered Dreams* (New York: Dell Publishing, 1987), p. 87.

[2] *Ibid.*, p. 163.

6. Hurt and Anger
[1] Dr. Susan Forward and Joan Torres, *Men Who Hate Women and the Women Who Love Them* (New York: Bantam Books, 1986), pp. 43, 46.

9. The Codependent Christian
[1] Robert S. McGee, *The Search for Significance*. 2nd ed. (Houston and Dallas, TX: Rapha Publishing/Word, Inc., 1990), pp. 55-60.

10. Identity: A Sense of Worth
[1] Robert S. McGee, Jim Craddock, Pat Springle, *Your Parents and You*. Edited by Susan Joiner. (Houston and Dallas, TX: Rapha Publishing/Word, Inc., 1990), p. 3.

[2] *The Search for Significance* and *Your Parents and You* can be obtained either at your local Christian bookstore, or by writing: Rapha Publishing, P.O. Box 580355, Houston, TX, 77258.

11. Lordship: A Sense of Belonging
[1] For an explanation of manipulative control as idolatry, see John N. Oswalt, *The Book of Isaiah* (Grand Rapids: Eerdmans, 1986), pp. 82-89.

[2] Beattie, *Codependent No More*, p. 200.

14. Three Ingredients: No. 2: Detach
[1] Beattie, *Codependent No More*, p. 58.

16. Emerging
[1] Elisabeth Kübler-Ross, *On Death and Dying* (New York: MacMillan Publishing, 1969).

18. The Reality of God
[1] Paul G. Hiebert, "The Flaw of the Excluded Middle," *Missiology: An International Review*, Vol. X. No. 1, (Jan. 1982), pp. 35-47.

[2] Simon Kistemaker, *The Parables of Jesus* (Grand Rapids: Baker Book House, 1980), p. 31.

20. Three Stages of Growth
[1] The author thanks Melanie Ahlquist and staff members of the Texas Area Campus Crusade for Christ for their insights on the three stages of growth.